Advance Praise for *Leading Out Loud*

"For those remarkable leaders who have the capacity to inspire, communications is less of a rote skill and more of a life practice in creating meaning. *Leading Out Loud* encourages us to plumb the depths of our own motivations in order to communicate change with the power that only authenticity engenders."
—Randy Komisar, virtual CEO, adjunct faculty, Stanford University, author, *The Monk and the Riddle*

"This is a powerful, simple, and essential tool for any leader who hopes to move and inspire others. Keep it on your desk."
—Patrick Lencioni, author, *The Five Dysfunctions of a Team*

"This book will make you laugh, cry, and squirm. It will inspire you and it may even scare you. Implementing Terry's advice may require far more courage and discipline than anything else you do as a leader, but if you want to know and do something for yourself that will enrich your character and engage your spirit, then read and use the ideas in *Leading Out Loud*."
—Jim Kouzes, coauthor, *The Leadership Challenge*, chairman emeritus of the Tom Peters Company

"Pearce has written a gem. *Leading Out Loud* is a superb, enjoyable, and practical road map on how we can become effective inspirers of change. Read it and act on it!"
—Costas Markides, Robert Bauman Professor of Strategic Leadership, London Business School

"*Leading Out Loud* will become an oft-turned-to handbook when stress is high and the outcome of particular communication is critical."
—Mel Bergstein, founder and CEO, Diamond Cluster

"Terry Pearce reminds us of the engaging storyteller, or the favorite college teacher. But that's just the point. He teaches us to discard the rhetoric of many public communications, replacing it with something far more powerful: the simple and genuine human voice. *Leading Out Loud*'s teachings will change its readers as well as those they lead."
—John Hammergren, chairman and CEO,
  McKesson Corporation

"*Leading Out Loud* is clear, compelling, and comprehensive. Pearce eloquently demonstrates that authenticity is the fundamental success trait of both men and women leaders."
—Judy B. Rosener, professor, Graduate School of Management, University of California, Irvine, and author, "Ways Women Lead" (*Harvard Business Review*)

"Drawing from a wealth of personal experience and the perspective of his unique skybox on leadership practices and effective leaders, Terry Pearce gives an authentic voice to the critical role of leaders in realizing change. This book is like a GPS system for leaders. It points the way, giving clear and practical advice on how to achieve results through clear and deep communication."
—Jim Hornthal, founder, Preview Travel, Lester Fellow for Entrepreneurship, University of California, Berkeley

Leading Out Loud

Leading Out Loud

Inspiring Change Through Authentic Communication

New and Revised Edition

Terry Pearce

Foreword by David S. Pottruck

JOSSEY-BASS
A Wiley Imprint
www.josseybass.com

Published by Jossey-Bass
A Wiley Imprint
989 Market Street, San Francisco, CA 94103-1741   www.josseybass.com

Jossey-Bass books and products are available through most bookstores. To contact Jossey-Bass directly
call our Customer Care Department within the U.S. at 800-956-7739, outside the U.S. at 317-572-3986,
or fax 317-572-4002.

Jossey-Bass also publishes its books in a variety of electronic formats. Some content that appears in
print may not be available in electronic books.

Library of Congress Cataloging-in-Publication Data

Pearce, Terry, 1941-
   Leading out loud : inspiring change through authentic communication /
Terry Pearce ; foreword by David S. Pottruck.-New and rev. ed.
      p. cm.
Includes bibliographical references and index.
   ISBN 0-7879-6397-6 (alk. paper)
   1. Leadership. 2. Communication in management. 3. Public speaking.
I. Title.
   HD57.7.P4 2003
   658.4'092—dc21   2003000855

Printed in the United States of America
SECOND EDITION
HB Printing   10 9 8 7

To
Jaymee McKenna Pearce
Austin James Ehrlicher

and to
Sarah Polster

Contents

Foreword

I met Terry Pearce in 1993, when he was working on the first edition of *Leading Out Loud*. I had just become president of Schwab. I wasn't really qualified, but my predecessor had a heart attack and I happened to be the best person available at the time. It was an enormous "field promotion."

I swiftly realized I was in over my head; all too soon that became a widely held perception. I thought I needed a speechwriter to help me communicate my leadership style and my vision for our future. By good fortune an acquaintance introduced me to Terry Pearce. I quickly learned that I didn't need a speechwriter. What I needed was a leadership coach, a mentor, and a confidant—and that's what I got. Terry and I began a ten-year journey of exploring and implementing a new and effective model of leadership communication. Within Schwab, and to me personally, the lessons of *Leading Out Loud* and the principle of authenticity in leadership communication that Terry teaches have made a world of difference. We have incorporated this model as part of our core competencies for leadership, and it has served us equally well in all the rapid and dramatic cycles of growth and contraction in the last decade.

Before this journey, I believed that the measurement of good leadership communication was the thunderous applause at the end of a speech, the smiles I could see in the front row, my jokes getting a laugh rather than a groan, and hearing later that people enjoyed it. I now understand that great leadership communication includes everything—the first testing of an idea, the informal conversations, the e-mail and voice mail, the late-night sessions with a strategy team. All these are based on an intricate and personally crafted message platform and a willingness to engage with others, openly and fully.

What sets this edition of *Leading Out Loud* apart from the first edition and from all the other leadership communication books is that it starts at the true beginning. The issue is not just constructing a good speech. The first issue is deciding what you want to say, what you need to say, and why you want to say it. Before you can construct a message, you have to find your passion, your courage, and your authentic self; then you must be prepared to reveal them in the context of your organization, your strategy, and your circumstances.

The message platform includes more than facts and more than just good ideas. It includes the statement of the change that is needed, the values that will be better expressed when that change is implemented, the personal motivation of the leader, the leader's vision for the future, and more. Until that platform is built, good speeches are just that: good speeches. After the platform is built, a speech becomes only one element in communicating the need for change in a way that inspires everyone, including the leader.

The willingness and ability to engage with others makes all the difference to the leader of the new century. Until you have mastered the emotional strength to include others fully, communication is not complete. These are the lessons that Terry has tried to teach me over the years. They are the lessons he has taught other business leaders, executives, managers, graduate students, and political figures around the world.

In this edition, Terry addresses all forms of communication thoroughly and as the continuum they are. The person trying to be inspirational in a speech is the same leader who sends out forty e-mail notes a day and chairs five meetings. If they appear to be two different people, that just won't work. Entertaining people certainly helps get their attention, but it's the message and the leader's personal engagement with the message that will inspire commitment and action. This lesson and how we raise our game to this level comprise the messages of *Leading Out Loud*.

None of this is easy. You cannot just read a book, hear a lecture, or pass a test to master the craft. Like most important skills, leadership communication demands work. If you want to take your leadership *impact* to new heights, you must undertake leadership communication with a good deal of personal introspection and with all your heart and soul.

It's hard work—and this new edition serves as the best guide you can get. It is a guide for everyone, not just those who sit in corner offices, to find and express the changes that they might want to champion. Terry presents two fundamental precepts. The first half is about what it takes to lead in this time of ubiquitous information and strong passions. Terry shows why leadership is now both more personal and more public than ever, and how an aspiring leader can deal with both aspects. The second half is a marvelous toolbox of practicalities. It provides a framework and all the questions anyone would need to really explore to construct their own message of change.

To me, this is an entirely new work. It will teach you about real leadership *and* about real leadership communication; how to look inside yourself to figure out what you are all about; how to find, follow, and employ the source of your passion; how to commit yourself to being a force for change, and ultimately how to inspire others to do the same. In this world of cynicism, the lessons Terry teaches are as timely as they are timeless.

If your field is business, you don't need to be the CEO to begin employing these lessons and principles. Department heads, divisional heads, and regional vice presidents can all put these principles to work. Moreover, staff members who are aspiring to these jobs and other roles in middle or senior management would do well to spend time with *Leading Out Loud* and begin to prepare. You never know when a "field promotion" might be in store for you. If you are in any other profession, or if you are only tentatively exploring your chance to make a difference in the world, the lessons are equally useful.

I have been really lucky over the past ten-plus years. I've been able to receive coaching and counsel directly from Terry Pearce. This book is the next best thing. For tomorrow's aspiring leaders (and today's leaders who want to raise their game), *Leading Out Loud* is worthy of your time and energy. Read it and then read it again and again. Then apply what you've learned. Believe me, you will be richly rewarded.

February 2003   DAVID S. POTTRUCK
San Francisco, California

Preface

In the first version of *Leading Out Loud*, I presented my understanding of what inspires people to act and offered a guide to writing and delivering an authentic and inspiring speech. I focused on how leaders could develop and deliver the first outward expression of a leadership message, and suggested that authenticity was at the core of leadership, fundamental to its practice and pivotal to success.

Shortly after the book's publication in 1995, the principles of *Leading Out Loud* were incorporated into an intensive executive course on authentic leadership communication. Participants in the course come to understand the personal nature of leadership and focus on the development of a message platform, not merely a speech. This requires introspection, courage, and persistence. It requires finding and building the courage to give voice to the change message and developing the skill of connecting with others in a way that will inspire them to engage with the ideas and passion of the leader.

This program has engaged thousands of leaders and potential leaders of all stripes in all parts of the world. Through the coursework, my classes at the Haas School of Business and the London Business School, and my work with individuals, I have seen leaders emerge, each from their own crucible of life, to find new ways of expressing themselves. I consider myself fortunate to have helped in that process.

My thinking, my presentations, and the material of the course have all been modified, enhanced, and enriched with examples from these experiences as well as from world affairs. This edition of *Leading Out Loud* reflects all of that work and change. The application of its principles has broadened from speeches to the wider range of leadership communication, extending beyond the "big speech" to daily communication and interactions, including e-mail, voice mail, meetings, interviews, question-and-answer sessions, and one-on-one conversations. I've learned that the fundamental principles of message development and communication apply in all forums and media, and that leaders must communicate change initiatives broadly and frequently. I've learned a great deal about how clarity and depth of communication interplay; I've learned that without depth, clarity is sterile and inadequate to inspire change. I've learned that the critical factors in the effectiveness of communication, other than the cogency of the content, are the leaders' authenticity and their effectiveness in successfully deploying their Selves in a variety of ways. This edition puts a much broader scope on the development of a leadership message, using it not only in preparation for a speech but also as the platform for every communication that you, as a leader, might have about change.

Four questions were central to these broader applications:

- What elements make a message about change complete?
- How do we actually connect with one another?
- What principles can a leader apply to inspire others to action?
- How can we learn to communicate in the moment without moving to the natural defaults of defensiveness and manipulation or demands for compliance?

Pondering these questions revealed useful distinctions that can measure our effectiveness as leaders and these distinctions apply to communication. Your ability to *manage* is measured by what you know and what you get done, but your ability to *lead* is measured not only by your competence but also by your ability to communicate who you are and what you stand for. With this kind of core distinction, we can more easily define what is central to leadership communication. We can see what distinguishes it from other forms of communication—and can expand and deepen our skills.

After the publication of *Leading Out Loud*, I was told by many friends and some casual readers that the book was too deeply personal; that it would not gain a following. I saw that as a risk—a risk that I accepted and wanted to take. After thirty years of experience, I believe that leadership *is*, at its core, a personal pursuit. It always manifests itself in communication, first in a declaration about a new order of things and then in the myriad of ways we connect with others and convey our personal strength of passion and conviction for the cause.

I can't go to Washington, D.C., without wending my way around the Tidal Basin to the Jefferson Memorial to reread his immortal words—"we hold these truths to be self-evident"—and to go on to the other quotations: "Institutions must advance also to keep pace with the times. We might as well require a man to wear still the coat which fitted him when a boy as civilized society to remain ever under the regimen of their barbarous ancestors." Jefferson was a child of the Enlightenment, and he knew that change was both difficult and necessary, and that it required a strength of communication equal to the import of the change to be brought about. His leadership created public possibilities that perhaps would not have been seen without him.

Jefferson's declarations came from his beliefs, his times, and his hopes for the future. They were deeply felt and very personal—and taken up personally by many others since. So yes, this is a personal book, as is the pursuit of change, as is the practice of leadership. It can be practiced by everyone with the awareness of their own place, a sense of their potential, and a conviction about changing the order of things, whatever the scale, whatever the venue.

What's New in This Edition?

In addition to expanding the scope of communication covered, this new edition also expands the principles that shift communication to a form that inspires. In the first edition, I suggested three such principles as primary: *discovering what matters*, *giving voice to values*, and *connecting with others*. In this edition, I expand on those ideas, adding an emphasis on discipline and suggesting a fourth principle: *deciding to lead*. The more I have worked with individual leaders and with groups at universities or in the Leading Out Loud™ executive program, the more I have come to appreciate that today's leadership environment requires a decision to develop the emotional intelligence to manage the Self and deploy it in very different ways. All two-year-olds and most teenagers are willing to tell you how they feel and what they think, but it isn't always inspirational. The work of Daniel Goleman has certainly informed some of this discussion and much of the practice of developing that intelligence and self-management, as has my work with clients, executives in the coursework, and graduate students who have taken it on themselves to grow in this way.

Because this edition focuses on the development of a message platform rather than a single speech, it has fewer examples from public figures than the first edition; it has more from clients and graduate students, many just emerging as leaders. This shift reflects the fact that now, with new communication tools, we have more individual power than ever. Change is not just being generated in boardrooms or in developed countries by people with economic power. The best organizations, the best leaders, are fostering new loci of power on every level, not just at the top. Self-expression thrives on information and a sense of one's ability to change things. The emergence of Internet cafés in nearly every country of the world makes it feasible for more and more people to see possibilities. Many people crave inspiring leadership to help make some of those possibilities real or, in some cases, to make sure that other, more negative possibilities don't see the light of reality.

I was recently interviewed for a CD series on leadership in the new century, and was asked by the host if we needed great problems to create more leaders. I thought the question a good one, as we were talking about the possibilities in everyone to lead (not just politicians and organizational leaders). The host was hinting that we needed crisis in the world—crisis of the magnitude of war, pestilence, or graft—to bring about leadership. Yet the very best leaders that I know are not in the public eye, and they are addressing problems on a relatively small scale. But talk to them, and you will hear about their particular issue as though it was a major crisis.

I responded to the question: "Yes, and there are plenty of crises around, aren't there? To everyone who desires a change badly enough to speak out, and then to take action, the status quo *is* a crisis, worthy of their thoughts, their voice, and their life's energy." To such individuals, their problem of choice is magnified by their personal values and experience into crisis proportion. There is, indeed, an opportunity for each of us to lead. My hope is that this book will be a useful tool for you in your search to find what matters and to communicate it in a way that creates what your values dictate should happen.

What's Here?

The book is divided into two parts. Part One speaks to the requirements for leadership in today's environment. Chapter One explores the changing context of leadership, the changing requisites to lead effectively, and makes new distinctions of leadership communication that set the stage for the rest of the book. Chapters Two through Four discuss the principles of authentic leadership: discovering what matters, applying courage and discipline, and deciding to lead. These principles frame and define leaders as individuals, identifying what they will stand for, and how they will learn and practice communicating from their own values and from a base of emotional intelligence.

Part Two is a discussion of leadership communication itself. It details the ways in which we connect, and presents a framework that will help you construct a complete message platform for a change that you wish to lead. Chapter Five explains the skill-based principle of connecting with others. It discusses the nature of human connection, how our brains and bodies respond to various kinds of input from a would-be leader, and an explanation of the "magic three" of analogy and metaphor, story, and personal experience as the conveyors of grounded understanding, and therefore of inspiration.

In Chapters Six through Ten, I provide a template or framework as an organizational structure for building a complete message. The framework will help you ask the relevant questions so that you can fully convey your message. Chapter Six discusses the six basic blocks for building a relationship with listeners that conveys trustworthiness and competence. Chapter Seven describes the value of creating shared context to help you understand the history of the issue, as a relief for the change that you want to effect, and to build the foundation for your change scenario as a priority. Chapter Eight suggests ways to imagine, declare, and then describe the future in a way that is compelling, so others might see their role. Chapter Nine looks at the conclusion of any leadership message—the time to commit to action—and includes ways of measuring yourself for the effectiveness of inspiration in your message. Chapter Ten discusses various communication channels, starting with the speech as declaration and moving through models for question and answer situations, and how a leader can use them all to elicit an authentic response. In closing, the Epilogue emphasizes the current need to break with convention and practice authentic leadership communication—every day and in every situation—to satisfy the growing need for meaning, for ourselves and others.

Two appendixes supplement the material in the text. The first provides information on the choice and use of evidence in leadership communication. The second discusses personal performance appraisals, as well as ongoing communication with e-mail and other electronic methods, suggesting that these forums can all be used to gain engagement and commitment, rather than merely pique people's curiosity or demand compliance.

Who Should Read This Book?

The new times and the new communication tools have made leaders accessible, vulnerable, and visible. It takes more courage than ever to take the lead in changing things for the better. It may seem an inconvenience to have to communicate effectively every day; certainly doing so demands attention and time. But to those who want to lead, it is imperative.

You don't have to sit in the corner office to benefit from this book. If you feel deeply about the need for progress in any field, or if you want to discover more about how people emerge to lead change, *Leading Out Loud* will prove valuable to you.

Every book worth reading is an advocacy for change, a fine-tuned theme weaving its way through words, sentences, and paragraphs, helping the reader create a tapestry of personal change, of being altered for the better for having read it. My hope is that as you read and apply the themes of this edition of *Leading Out Loud,* your self-knowledge, conviction, and courage to make a difference in the world are enhanced to the point of action; or if you already have such conviction, that your ability to inspire is reawakened and improved to a degree that surprises you. *Leading Out Loud* provides principles, examples, and a method of being a conscious and effective inspirer of change. Please use it to stir others to join in creating progress in your world.

February 2003   TERRY PEARCE
Larkspur, California

PART ONE

Leadership Communication

Clear and Deep

Leading in today's world requires communication that is substantially different from what was needed only a decade ago. Leaders still communicate the facts, the information that is necessary to make and implement a decision. For this, leaders must be logical, suggesting that moving from where we are to where we are going is a needed, cogent, and doable change. But they also must constantly communicate the "why" that makes the action meaningful. Whether they are heading up a volunteer effort, a business, a club, a theater, an orchestra, a city, or a country, leaders must include the emotional and the spiritual implications of the actions they advocate. They have to acknowledge the impact of the changes they propose on those who will implement them. Such changes affect the way people feel and the way people interpret the meaning of their own participation. Such integrated communication not only conveys consistency with the strategy of the organization, it also suggests consistency with the values.

To inspire, communication has to express the competence of the communicator while also contributing to a sense of trust. Leaders have to be clear not just about the alignment of change with the organization's goals but also about their own stake in the change—why it is important to them personally. By communicating in this integrated way, leaders prove themselves both competent and trustworthy.

Four principles need to be employed to develop the capacity for such authentic leadership communication. The first three—discovering what matters, applying courage and discipline, and deciding to lead—are about "leading." These principles form the basis for developing a message platform for change, and they are the focus of Part One. The fourth principle, connecting with others, will provide the framework for Part Two.

1

The Changing Context for Leadership

I've been involved in leadership and communication for more than thirty years, first as a student leader, then as a corporate executive, a citizen diplomat, and finally as a coach and university teacher in the field. During my experience at International Business Machines in the early 1970s, my concept of leadership was one of directing the work, and I did it well. It was only as I left IBM and dipped a toe into the world of international diplomacy that I realized the extent to which inspiration contributes to any leader's effectiveness. In politics, and particularly in geopolitics, others don't have to follow your orders in order to survive. Cross-cultural issues are the perfect crucible for the creation and refinement of leadership skills and behaviors.

I observed such leadership close up for most of the 1980s, and carefully cataloged its successes and failures. As the cold war came to an end and the tenets of democracy and capitalism spread around the globe, I had high hopes for the reemergence of leaders who could take us on new and wonderful journeys, especially with the examples of Vaclav Havel and Nelson Mandela at the fore.

Instead, we have seen a continual erosion in the effectiveness of political and business leaders. Despite some exceptions, the trend is unmistakable. People in positions of power abuse that power, and we are left with few to trust, few to follow. The number of people who can inspire us is dwindling, and we feel it. In 1994, there were more than two thousand books in print on the subject of leadership.

For three years, from 1994 to 1997, the U.S. Congress authorized $10 million to develop "new generations of leaders in the areas of national and international affairs," and called for papers from academic institutions to accomplish that purpose. The best leadership consultants are commanding more than $10,000 per day from corporations, and there are few complaints about value.

The basic requirements of leadership have been defined consistently from the late John Gardner in the 1960s to Warren Bennis in the 1990s. Leaders see what is needed and inspire others to take action to effect change.

But just as this fundamental definition of leadership has been constant, the entire world in which we operate has been erratic. It seems we are at the edge of a social and psychological chasm. Those who would lead are confronting this abyss personally, as are each of their potential followers. Seeing what is needed and inspiring others are both growing ever more complex, and because of the dynamic of our global society that drives us to compete, fewer and fewer people even consider these as possible. In particular, fewer people of good will and great intention are willing to subject themselves to the fire walk of public leadership. And for those who do, the elements are more difficult than ever.

Seeing Needed Change

It is not as easy as it was to see what is needed. The change that is now required for success in many institutions is no longer merely incremental, it is discontinuous, radical, and frightening to those who participate. In fields as diverse as economics, medicine, biological and physical research, social and political structures, and certainly business, we are not simply being asked to "do better" than our predecessors, we are being asked to "do different." Leaders are faced with inspiring followers to take this same kind of risk; to jump this chasm with them. Since the first edition of Leading Out Loud, this chasm has broadened as a result of the dramatic up and down of the Internet market bubble, the renewed focus on the radical ends of the ideological, political, and religious spectra, and the acceleration of violence in disagreements at all levels.

A leader's ability to call for change is complicated further by general instability in the world. No promises of permanence are believable. We have seen physical and intellectual boundaries disappearing with increasing speed. These include chaos theory in science, wholesale changes in the map of the world, the redefinition of the family, changes in the relative roles of men and women, and—with the mapping of the human genome—an entirely new range of possibility with regard to what it means to be "human." All of these and more suggest fluid movement that defies understanding or rationalization. We no longer have the illusory security of the cold war, which provided boundaries that allowed countless world political figures the luxury of a predefined field on which to lead.

Certainly, the institution of business is feeling this same pressure. In the past fifteen years, capitalist companies around the world have had to turn their organizations into more responsive institutions, changing the very core of employment stability in a company. What was secure work in the old world is now frequently defined out of existence. Many large and prominent companies with strong cultures of employee-centric policies are yielding to the fiscal realities of the fast-moving pace of change. Hewlett-Packard, IBM, and, most prominently, the giants of the communications industry are routinely cutting back their workforces and moving operations to lower-cost locales at the cost of employee loyalty.

In the United States, people's confidence in their future is once again eroding. After a period of euphoria, the realism of the political and financial situation has returned people's view of the future close to that of the fall of 1994, when the director of the University of Michigan's Consumer Survey summarized the anxiety and insecurity gripping much of the population: "For the first time in fifty years, we are recording a decline in people's expectations, and their uncertainty and anxiety grow the farther you ask them to look into the future."[1] As of this writing, that assessment is being mirrored by the survey of consumer confidence of the Conference Board. In fact, in 2003, the index stood well below its base year of 1985. Job, career, and company no longer offer security. Anyone who wants to lead must offer stability of a new kind, a stability that does not come from these traditional forms.

In sum, the forces at play in the world portend a loss of control in our own destinies. In his 2001 book, *Between Two Ages*, Van Wishard points to three primary drivers of the escalation of anxiety: globalization, a new stage of technology development, and a long-term psychological and spiritual reorientation. Wishard is a futurist who bases his analysis on six thousand years of history. From that perspective, he suggests that globalization is "possibly the most ambitious collective human experiment in history," that the new stage of technology has as its objective to "supplant human meaning and significance," and that the effect of the psychological and spiritual reorientation is a worldwide "weakening of the structures that organize and regulate our life—religion, self-government, education, culture and the family."[2]

These trends are not just theoretical; they are at work in all of us and are shaking our ideas and belief systems to the core.

So the part of leadership that is "the vision thing" is not as simple as it used to be. Most of the boundaries that we've assumed for the past several decades are gone. Yet defining the proper direction is one primary responsibility of the leader of this century. The other is to communicate in a way that transforms change to progress in the minds of those who listen; to inspire them to act. That isn't easy either.

Breathing Life into Others

Would-be followers, people who might have perceived themselves as powerless, confront the same barriers as the would-be leaders, and they are also prone to cynicism about leadership in general. At the same time that their metaphorical walls are crumbling from events seemingly controlled by others, individuals are gaining new tools for building new boundaries themselves. The Internet and the growth of wireless communication have combined to create the most empowering toolbox since the invention of the telephone, and will have even broader impact. The network makes it possible for each of us to communicate opinions and other information to a web of recipients. It allows us to hold any individual leader's feet to the fire—and any company's as well—on matters of integrity. Because the network allows instant communication with multitudes of others, perceived breaches of integrity can be communicated instantly and broadly.

Perhaps the central and most challenging aspect of the spread of democracy and the triumph of capitalism is the promulgation of a subjective view of life. In all of human enterprise, in every community and business, we are growing more convinced that we have much more individual control than we thought before, and therefore more responsibility. Our elected officials, our CEOs, our educators, even our stockbrokers are telling us through word and deed that it is really up to us, not them, to make our life meaningful and prosperous. This new awakening is causing us to either isolate or to look for the solution to social ills from within ourselves and the community rather than from government bureaucrats; to ask for business solutions from individual workers or from ourselves rather than waiting for instructions from some CEO. Gen Xers are far more likely to start something on their own, to eschew large organizations. We can actually count on individuals volunteering to do their part to rid streets of drug dealers. We can look to citizens to be responsible for their health habits that may lead to serious illness. We can tap the knowledge and skill of individual workers to be more effective. But all this is only possible if we are inspired to do so. We can isolate, or we can engage.

The possibility for participation in life has advantages that Margaret Wheatley has illustrated with a metaphor from quantum physics:

> In the traditional model, we leave the interpretation of information to senior or expert people. . . . [These] few people, charged with interpreting the data, are, in fact, observing only very few of the potentialities contained within that data. . . . [But if] the wave of information spreads out broadly everywhere in the organization . . . many moments of meeting—

hundreds, even thousands of them will occur. . . . Instead of losing so many of the potentialities . . . [we will see] many of these potentials . . . [and be able to] discuss, combine, and build on them. . . . It would seem that the more participants we engage in this participative universe, the more we can access its potentials and the wiser we can become.[3]

The "wave of information" has increased exponentially since Wheatley wrote this paragraph in the early 1990s. But her metaphor continues to ring true, because it casts the problem and solution as the release of energy *from engagement rather than instruction*. Interconnectedness makes it difficult to see the change needed to enhance corporate or community performance, and it is even more challenging to inspire others to follow with enthusiastic action. People will do as they are told to meet the requirements of their jobs and to protect their families, but they will no longer be loyal to a leader who merely provides better information than they can get from someone else.

To inspire, the new leader must authentically engage in the issue at hand. To give a commitment, we have to have more than the information that would-be leaders provide. We must trust the leaders themselves.

The Effect of Media and Technology

Television, computers, and telecommunication technology have contributed to a central irony. While our overuse of media, voice mail, and electronic communication has *maximized* our need for authenticity, the requirements for "professionalism" in the use of media and the premium we put on instant and continuous information have *minimized* the possibility for real human connection. We may want to be in touch with the *real* person, but the one we see on television or hear on radio has already been scrubbed clean with the steel wool of a script, makeup, rehearsal, voice lessons, and all the other fixes that can be applied to effect perfection. Dialects, errors, and other human foibles that are so much a part of the authentic self are absent. Even with a "live" performance, technological aids mask the professional communicator. On October 6, 1993, the London *Times* described the use of the TelePrompTer, a system of transparent screens positioned to the side and in front of a speaker, presenting a script for easy reading. The device has been used for years in politics and is now spreading to the world of business communication. The author, Matthew Parris, ends the article on point: "We [the public] unconsciously recognize media-speak, and discount it, keeping the information it conveys at arm's length. We have a special compartment for talking heads. In Brighton last week, John Prescott, in a speech which was almost gibberish, lit a fire in the hearts of his audience which seemed unmerited by anything he said. He did so because he was answering a great, unconscious public hunger for *direct communication from our . . . leaders*" (emphasis mine).[4]

Prescott has gone on to become deputy prime minister of Great Britain; perhaps a coincidence, perhaps not.

If authenticity evades the professional communicator, so too, it evades those who embrace e-mail as their sole or even primary means of communicating. Can e-mail or voice mail, by themselves, inspire? Experience would suggest that they cannot, especially when they are used as the primary means to communicate. In an article for *Harvard Business Review*, Edward Hallowell, a psychiatrist and an instructor at Harvard Medical School, claims that the "human moment," a face-to-face interaction, is needed to avoid a predominance of worry that flows from the ambiguity of words or instructions unaccompanied by subtle meaning.[5] We need to know the emotion behind a communication. The growing use of *emoticons*, small electronic symbols to represent smiles, frowns, and even chagrin is evidence of the need, but no number of these clever symbols can replace a human smile, or for that matter, a real showing of disgust.

Our hunger for authentic communication will simply grow. We all know that floating somewhere in the atmosphere of virtual reality, television fantasy, and print media that urge us on to perfection, there is the deep meaning of the real world—the one with warts, mistakes, grief, and passion. We also know that lurking in the e-mail is the spirit of the writer, lost and wandering in the digital forest. In our lack of other means of remaining stable, we are recognizing the value of the firm ground of the authentic human connection. It is the only ground we will truly trust.

Business's need for creativity and participation is propelling us toward the authentic as well. Good management practice has moved from a purely external analysis of the business as an entity to a focus on the internal motivation of the individuals *in* the company. With this movement has come a greater requirement for leadership that recognizes and values deeper human needs, where leaders are closer to workers, more communicative and more vulnerable.

Where will the trend take us? The talent that business now needs to compete in the world economy can only come from greater fulfillment of employees at work. The successful companies of the next hundred years require leaders who are actually engaged in the process themselves, who continue to set the pace and direction from the front—and who are also in the middle, encouraging themselves and others to learn and change more rapidly.

The Case for Authenticity

In this context, personal communication is once again being recognized as a vital leadership skill. Charles Handy, former executive, lecturer, futurist, and professor at the London Business School, writes clearly about the need for authenticity in the coming age. "Integrity," says Handy, "comes naturally if you live for your vision. In other words, the vision cannot be something thought up in the drawing office. To be real, it has to come from the deepest parts of you, from an inner system of belief. The total pragmatist cannot be a transforming leader."[6] Like most thinkers in the field of leadership development, Handy recognizes that being aware of one's own convictions, being true to them in advocacy, and acting consistently with those convictions are *all* required to gather committed followers.

Natural Life, Natural Language, Natural Fire

Authenticity calls us to respond. A graduation speaker at a small college in Oregon recently told a story that illustrates the difference between authentic speech and informative speech. As the story goes, Sir Charles Laughton was attending a Christmas party with a large family in London. Well into the evening, the host decided that each person in attendance should read or recite a favorite passage, one that reminded them most of the Spirit of Christmas.

Laughton's turn came near the end, and he recited, in his beautifully trained voice, the Twenty-Third Psalm. Everyone applauded his effort, and the process continued. Within a few minutes, all had participated except one elderly aunt, who had dozed off in one corner of the room. She was particularly loved, and they gently woke her, explained what was going on, and asked her to take part. She thought for a moment, and then began in her shaky voice, "The Lord is my shepherd, I shall not want. . . ." The room hushed as she continued, and when she finished, tears were dripping down every face.

Upon leaving, one of the younger members of the family thanked Laughton for coming, and remarked on the difference in the response of the family to the two "readings." In one case, appreciation; in the other, deep connection and involvement. "How do you account for it?" asked the young man, shaking his head. Laughton looked at him and replied simply, "I know the Psalm . . . she knows the Shepherd."

The beloved aunt was not planning her recitation; it grew from a ground that was far deeper than any plan to impress the audience. She found, on her own, the proper experience that allowed her to slip into her *real* skin for the occasion; indeed, she never slipped out of it.

Authenticity is hard to develop and even harder to coach. Since authenticity is a *way of being* as a leader rather than *things you do* as a leader, few instructions are outwardly helpful. Consultants revert to "just be yourself," which is instantly interpreted as "act like you would like yourself to act." Of course, doing so has little resemblance to being oneself.

The responsibility for authenticity, then, belongs to you, the leader. Through a combination of introspection and discipline, you have to find your authentic voice and amplify it so that it resonates with those who follow you. Such introspection and discipline applied to communication can even become a regimen for leadership as a whole. A coach can only advise you where to look, and then recognize and call your attention to your success. Consider the following example:

In the spring of 1994, Dave Pottruck, then president of The Charles Schwab Corporation, was planning to speak to two hundred members of the company's management team about changes that were occurring in the organization. Like many companies, Schwab had recently instituted substantial alterations in its structure and in the way it did business. Dave was to speak about two significant events: the move of nearly five hundred people from the West Coast to the mountain states, and the institution of "Saturday hours," which involved keeping the branch offices open for four hours on the weekend to serve customers better. He had prepared his speech to spell out all the details of both moves. He would outline the rationale behind the changes, look at the increased business that the firm expected, comment on the efficiencies that would result, and finally describe the future of this growing firm and explain what such growth could mean to everyone in the room.

An excellent communicator, Dave had done a beautiful job of composing the outline of the evidence. The audience was going to get all the facts they needed to be convinced of the business viability of the changes. He had planned to open his talk this way: "I am excited about speaking with you tonight regarding the changes we have planned. Saturday hours and the new concentration in the mountain states will make us even more responsive to our customers. As we grow into the next decade, we will be seeing similar changes for the same reason . . . to serve our customers better while we provide more leverage for our own growth."

At that point, Dave and I had been working together for more than a year. He called me two weeks before the event to consult on his remarks. When we considered the likely impact of the speech on the audience, we concluded that all the managers would happily *comply* with the changes. But for them to execute the changes with the enthusiasm and dedication of a family, as Dave wanted, he knew he needed the *full commitment* of the management team.

We focused on what the speech could do to galvanize the audience behind the moves, to let people know that they were valued, and to gain their commitment to follow his lead. Dave eventually began his remarks like this:

> When I decided to speak to all of you about these changes, I was quite excited. As you know, we have been considering both the relocation to the mountain states and opening the branches for a few hours on Saturday for some time. But as I reflected on the impact of these changes, it occurred to me that the relocation did not require me to move from *my* home, and in fact, *I* was not going to work any more time on Saturday than I already do. My kids are used to my irregular hours, yet know that I still value my time with their sports teams and the other weekend time we have together. For many of you an occasional Saturday away from the family will be something new, and certainly, these changes will cause some disruption in the family patterns of your staffs.
>
> It also occurred to me that *I* wasn't going to be telling my staff about moving or working Saturdays. Rather, *I* get to address the big issues, while *you* will be conveying the news to individuals and dealing with their very specific questions.
>
> Given these thoughts, I quickly realized that you might not be as excited about these moves as I am, even though these changes are for the good of the company and ultimately will create more opportunity for all of us.
>
> So this evening, I want to outline the rationale for the changes, let you know what tremendous effort has gone into the business planning, and speak for just a moment about the impact these changes will ultimately have on our company's

growth rate. Then I also want to spend some time discussing the considerations we all went through about the personal impact on you and your families. Many of you have been involved in this planning.

After that, I'd like to deal with as many questions as you have, and listen to any further ideas you might have to make it easier for all of us to realize the benefits with a minimum of disruption.

These changes in his remarks did nothing to alter the logical content of the speech or the eventual action of the managers, yet the new version set an entirely different tone and required something entirely new from Dave. He was not only going to engage his *mind* for the talk, he was also going to reflect on the *meaning* of the subject to himself and to his audience. By engaging both his mind and his heart, he could engage both the mind and heart of the audience. Doing so altered how Dave was able to talk and listen about this subject in the more informal and more critical follow-up situations with employees. By looking not just at the practical but at the real human impact of the changes on himself and his audience, he was able to relate his own experience and to connect authentically with the group of managers. We made similar changes throughout the message, retaining the logic and strength of the explanations and adding elements that required Dave's deeper reflection and specificity—and that would evoke that same response from the audience.

The day following the speech, Dave invited me to listen to the voice mail from some who had heard him. The remarks did not merely compliment the speech, they complimented the man. Whereas the original speech allowed him to direct a corporation, the final product allowed him to lead the people in a company, a distinction that is at the heart of our changing business and political environment. Because Dave had done the reflection, this same attitude of understanding and inclusivity began to permeate his other communication about these changes as well, and that change contributed substantially to his effectiveness as a leader.

We applied this same lesson many times during my ten-year tenure at Schwab, perhaps most dramatically in 1995, as we codified and communicated the company's vision, values, and strategic imperatives to all seven thousand employees. An opinion survey indicated that many were unclear on the company direction, did not trust senior management, and had serious doubts about their own career growth and their ability to contribute to the company. Over a ten-month period, through intense and authentic communication from the company's leadership, Schwab crossed a threshold from an enthusiastic corporation with a mission to become an aligned, focused, and committed group of people.

Between 1995 and 2002, the entire company engaged in this same process four times, and each time employees emerged inspired, reenergized, and rededicated to their customers, to their fellow employees, and particularly to the senior leadership of the company. The keys? The four requisites of authenticity: faithful attention to what matters, courageous voicing of those values in the context of business, development of the emotional intelligence to lead, and continual emphasis on not just competence but connection with other human beings.

Those executives and other leaders who already feel overtaxed by the demands of their publics may see these four requisites as yet more work—and not necessarily work they are ready to take on. Many choose to delegate drafting their communication about change to a professional staff. Some are concerned with the legal ramifications of every word they say, and with good reason. Our society has made it difficult to make even the most honest mistakes.

Ironically, the corporate and political worlds are spending millions to determine what inspires the real participation of people. For the past three decades, human resource and organizational behavior experts have been looking for exactly the right organizational form for our era. Metaphors as diverse as the "upside down triangle" and the "blueberry pancake" have been proposed as ideal models to finally "empower" people nearest the customer to make decisions. If I ever get to write an entire book about empowerment, it would be called *We've Spent Thirty Years Opening the Cage and Nobody Wants to Come Out*. Organizational structures don't create empowered behavior any more than the structure of marriage creates a long-term match. People contribute when they are inspired—and if they are inspired, they will ignore the organizational structure totally in order to do the right thing.

Communicating from the Inside Out

Is it possible to communicate authentically, from both the head and the heart, and still get things done? How do leaders touch their own deeper personal values? How do you communicate practical solutions from a place of greater substance and meaning?

As a leader, you can inspire commitment by looking inward first, by becoming aware of what you want to say, and by communicating a much more personal vision of the future, based on much more personal knowledge of the past and realistic experience in the present. Such a focus means initially ignoring potential followers in favor of personal passion. Leaders who develop their message only on the basis of what others might want invariably play to others and only try to please them. Focusing on the themes of your own consciousness is the real driver of what you have to say. Others' reaction to you will be different, depending on which focus of communication you choose. If you only perform to others' standards, they may be entertained, but if you start the communication process with your own passion, they will be excited, and they will grasp a new and real possibility from your own authentic experience.

2

Discover What Matters

I met Gary Fiedel at a spiritual retreat in the early 1980s. In quiet conversation, I learned that he was an accountant in a town very near to my own home, and I learned about his background in the streets of Brooklyn. Gary's were not the suburban streets, they were the streets that had walk-up apartments in the heart of Coney Island. When Gary was in his teens, he met some friends who had fairly rough ideas of what life was about. Within a few years, he was on a track that might well have ended in some kind of violence, perhaps in a Brooklyn pool hall or some other place of street worship.

During some particularly dangerous times, Gary had the good sense to visit his cousin who was a CPA on Long Island. Through what Gary says was "sheer good luck," he was able to apprentice with his cousin, and over the next few years to move to Northern California and set up his own small accounting practice. Gary married and had a son. The marriage ended in divorce, Gary went on a pre-midlife spiritual quest, and we ended up at the same retreat in the basement of a San Francisco church.

I shared a little of my own frustration with Gary. I too was divorced, and I too was in the very early stages of setting up a small business. But unlike Gary, I worried every day whether the ATM would give me the automatic $20. Aside from a little prayer that I said in front of that banking altar every couple of days, I had no controls over my cash flow or revenue stream.

A week after the retreat, Gary arrived unannounced at my office door, pulled a few files from the single-drawer cabinet and told me he would bring them back in a week. When he did, he delivered my first set of business reports, and gave me instructions to send him my cash receipts, my checkbook register, and my credit card bills every month. He said he would bill me when I could afford it.

This was an extraordinary act of faith and I never forgot it. I called Gary's house to thank him, and connected with an answering machine. The message was, "Hi, this is Gary, and this is not an answering machine, it is a questioning machine! The two questions are, 'Who are you?' and 'What do you want?'" Then there was a pause, and the message went on, "and if you think those are trivial questions, consider that 95 percent of the population goes through life and never answers either one!"

I have later heard that greeting attributed to various people, but it was Gary Fiedel's version that stuck with me. While I certainly had enough life experience to suggest that I was searching for the answers to those questions, I had never asked them explicitly. I was surprised and inspired by the power of the questions in my own life, and now, I find them indispensable to my work with leaders. Leaders simply must know their own values if they are to inspire others.

Who Are You? What Do You Want?

Experiencing conviction of what change is required calls for personal reflection—not merely reading good management books. An authentic vision for progress doesn't just appear out of the ether, nor does it progress from what *others* believe to be important. *Your* passion about what you want to change grows from the foundation of values that have been formed by your life experience. These values are vital to you personally, not because they are socially acceptable, although they might be—and certainly not because they look good on a plaque on the wall—but because you have actually experienced them to be true.

Warren Bennis, who has studied leadership longer than any other American scholar, continues to stress the need for such self-knowledge as a prerequisite to effectiveness as a change agent. When reflecting on his own performance as president of the University of Cincinnati, he found that when he was most effective it was "because I knew what I wanted." It was that experience that drew Bennis to define the first competency of leadership as the *"management of attention."*[1] He continued to stress this need for focus on the delineation of individual values: "Anyone who wants to express himself fully and truly must have a point of view. Leadership without perspective and point of view isn't leadership—and of course it must be your own perspective, your own point of view. You cannot borrow a point of view any more than you can borrow someone else's eyes. It must be authentic, and if it is, it will be original, because you are an original."[2]

I'm dismayed by the number of men and women I interview who have retired from leadership positions decrying their failure to take time for personal reflection while they were active in their posts. They have assumed positions in organizations that they did not found, and rather than initially considering the impact they might make on the organization and proceeding from a foundation of values, they have defined themselves as they went along. First, they accepted the old tenets of the organization, and then only gradually discovered what was important to them personally. This trial-and-error method of leadership results in an inconsistent message and a lack of commitment by those engaged in the enterprise.

Leaders who make a transition from an old set of dominant values to a set that reflects their own beliefs make a substantial mark on the organization. Those who do not make that transition become caretakers, and are often replaced when the first significant challenge faces the enterprise. John Sculley successfully made this transition at Apple. His successors Michael Spindler and Gil Amelio did not. Spindler was to put the financial ship right, while Amelio was to lead to new vision. Unfortunately, Amelio had no idea what he wanted to do at Apple before he assumed the leadership of this deeply passionate company. By the time he started to communicate his ideas nearly a year had gone by, and most of the early enthusiasm of a great number of dedicated people had drained out of the company. It took the return of Steve Jobs, the spiritual leader of the firm, to right it.

Lou Gerstner successfully made the transition at IBM. John Ackers did not. Ronald Reagan and Bill Clinton successfully made the transition as president of the United States. The interim president, George Bush Sr., did not.

These successful leaders spoke frequently and effectively about their convictions. Former New York Governor Mario Cuomo, arguably the best United States political communicator of the last two decades, reflects on his motivation to speak in his self-edited compendium *More Than Words*, "For me, the vital thing is that *there is something important I want to say.* . . . As I look back over the speeches I selected for this volume, I note that most of the things I was trying to say revolved around the *small cluster of basic ideas that have resonated with me for most of my adult life*" (emphasis mine).[3]

These core ideas (the rule of law, insistence on a sense of responsibility, the rejection of the melting pot for the mosaic view of our multiculturalism, the need for seeing our disparate society as a family, the belief that work is better than welfare, and the idea that economic growth is the provider of the American dream) are the topics for Cuomo's best-planned speeches, the ones he considers his most definitive. These topics formed the basis for his informal communication as well. They defined Cuomo as a leader.

You too will find that there are very few ideas that constitute the core of your philosophy. These principles are more than a point of view. They are the tenets you believe to be vital to address, the questions that you wrestle with intellectually and emotionally, and they probably represent the quandaries of your personal life as well—perhaps in different dress, but the same nonetheless. Delineating your point of view, then, is the first step toward communicating authentically. You don't have to write eloquent speeches, but you do have to develop and refine the message or messages that define you.

Simply put, a person who is not at least struggling with these questions of Who are you? and What do you want? just can't lead. Any message about significant change that you construct without reflection on its importance to you will not inspire you, and will therefore not inspire others. To engage in the search for answers to these questions, you don't have to look far. The answers are inside you, sometimes screaming to get out.

Recognizing and Reflecting on Your Point of View

Every idea that you hold passionately has a background in your personal experience. Two of the bases of predictive psychology are first, that our beliefs are a product of our past teachings, and second, that those things learned through actual experience and personal observations have more power to form our future than ideas learned by abstract examination.

The personal nature of our life path has roots in ancient lore. The Greeks claimed that the human life force was guided by "daimons" or attending spirits who defined each individual's destiny. Our daimon, believed the Greeks, invites us to certain life experiences and keeps us from others to further our development. James Hillman, today's most noted archetypal psychologist, compares this daimon to similar beliefs in other traditions: "Hindus speak of karma; Romans would have called this ghost your genius. . . . In our century, [the angel] has reappeared as Jung's 'Wise Old Man' and 'Wise Old Woman', who, Jung says, are 'configurations of the guiding Self.'"[4]

By contrast, much of today's psychology regards many of our most influential and powerful past experiences as occurrences to live down or recover from. Certainly recovery is sometimes needed; but our feelings, compassion, conviction, and dedication to study are strengthened by our entire past, both "good" and "bad" experiences. At the extreme, the most compassionate and effective counselors are those who have themselves experienced tragedy, addiction, or poverty, and the strongest leaders are those who have experienced or personally witnessed the negative effects of the status quo and the subsequent transformative power of change.

When I ask my graduate classes to identify leaders of any period who were the most effective at inspiring others, the lists are remarkably consistent. Nelson Mandela, Martin Luther King Jr., Joan of Arc, John F. Kennedy, Margaret Thatcher, Abraham Lincoln, Anwar Sadat. Several spiritual leaders are consistently mentioned as well: Gandhi, Mohammed, Jesus, Siddartha. What do these people have in common?

Without hesitation, the group responds with words like *passion*, *commitment*, and *self-knowledge*. Clearly, this group of leaders could communicate in a way that was authentic, from the basis of their real values, whether they were giving speeches or conversing informally. We use words like *called* or *fated* to describe the strength of their conviction, yet each of us has that calling, some louder than others, some more cluttered with other noise; but nonetheless, our daimon is calling us to life, to express ourselves.

Life Experiences That Define You

Therapists and spiritual healers start by searching for their subjects' defining moments, whether through hypnosis, regression, or other therapy. Without regard to the complexity of the intervention, the process is simple. Reflect on what has actually influenced your behaviors and attitudes. Identify those specific life experiences that you remember as significant, and then identify the value associated with that experience. If done with honesty, this kind of exercise will lead you to the basis for your own leadership, the fundamentals of a defining message, perhaps even to the institution within which you want to lead.

Howard Schultz found himself, at seven years old, with a father who had broken his leg on the job and a mother who took in washing from others just to make ends meet. He saw that his father had been worn down by the system . . . he had gone from one job to another, never having health insurance, and when he got hurt, he didn't work, and the family didn't eat. Schultz grew up to lead Starbucks, and he says in his biography:

> Years later, that image of my father—slumped on the family couch, his leg in a cast, unable to work or earn money, and ground down by the world—is still burned into my mind. Looking back now, I have a lot of respect for my dad. He never finished high school, but he was an honest man who worked hard. . . .
>
> The day he died, of lung cancer, in January 1988, was the saddest of my life. He had no savings, no pension. More important, he had never attained fulfillment and dignity from work he found meaningful.
>
> As a kid, I never had any idea that I would one day head a company. But I knew in my heart that if I was ever in a position where I could make a difference, I wouldn't leave people behind.[5]

What value did Schultz generate from this experience? The value of never leaving anyone behind, of creating a real sense of community. He grew up determined to create a place that would nurture those who worked there. As a result of that value, he successfully lobbied the SEC to grant stock to part-time Starbucks employees. Walk into any Starbucks and ask the employees behind the counter if they like working there and why, and you will see the reflection of Howard Schultz's image of his father on that couch. Most feel included. Few feel left behind.

Distilling Values into Conviction About Change

In my graduate school classes in leadership communication, each student spends an entire term developing a single message. I ask them to choose their topic by answering one of three sets of questions:

- What single value is so important that you would (will) teach it to your children as the most important foundation of a happy life?

- What condition in your chosen industry would you change and how?

- What is the most important social issue we have to deal with as a community (world, nation, state, or whatever)? How would you correct it?

Students are required to have had some personal experience in the issue that will illustrate how they formed their position on the subject.

Developing the message and communicating about these topics reveals some solid conviction in the students. Additionally, they realize before term's end that the topic questions are interlaced; that is, their *values* create their conviction, whether it is about the value itself or about one of the applications of the value in business or society. For example, one student, Rob Nicholsen, chose to speak about the preservation of the environment, imploring his audience of MBA candidates to take steps toward conservation of natural resources. This is a fairly common topic in California, where many people are environmentally conscious, especially on university campuses and perhaps particularly so at Berkeley. Accordingly, it is difficult to move an audience to further action; people believe they are already doing enough.

But Rob is not a typical conceptual environmentalist. A native of Canada, he related his own personal experience of observing lakes near his home town lose their fish population to acid rain. He quoted a space-shuttle astronaut's observation that there were only two man-made landmarks visible from space . . . the Great Wall of China and a massive old-growth clear-cut in his home province. He was highly credible as he had studied environmental science as an undergraduate, but he also made an authentic connection with his audience through his strong personal conviction—an outgrowth of his personal experience.

Rob could draw on his environmental experience to communicate metaphorically on business or political issues. The preservation of capital, the efficient use of by-products, the idea of personal responsibility for the greater good, these topics and others could be addressed using these same events to stimulate his own conviction. The strength of this message resulted from Rob's reflection on a single question, and his use of the answer to develop the message.

As you can imagine, contemplating your entire life story will often reveal not just one but an entire array of individual values as well as their relative importance. Accordingly, I ask each corporate and political client to write or dictate an autobiography as a first step toward learning to communicate authentically. I request that they pay particular attention to events in their past that seem like turning points, events that have prompted fundamental decisions about the relative importance of ideas, things, and behaviors. We then use these events to construct messages around fundamental themes, drawing out their authentic concerns.

In late 1994, I worked with the executive team of a small company, Taylor-Made Office Systems, to help them redefine their vision and values. I interviewed Barry Taylor, the founder and CEO, and discovered that he had been orphaned as a boy, started his business as a very young man, and delivered his product to customers from his own secondhand truck. In addition, he had been divorced twice and had tragically lost a teenage son in an accident. These events and his many specific vivid memories of them shaped his values.

Barry had grown his company to three hundred employees and nearly $150 million, but it still exemplified his basic values. Is it any wonder that he emphasizes a strong family feeling, independence, and the need to serve the customer above all else? To this entrepreneur, these values did not come from a quick read of popular management books, they came from his life, and they carried with them all the authenticity of his own passion and conviction.

Barry has since sold his original company, regrouped and started two others with the same fundamental values at their core.

Like Barry Taylor, Mario Cuomo, Howard Schultz, Rob Nicholsen, and every other leader who has effectively led change, each of us has something unique to say, and it is based on our particular make-up and our rich and sometimes dire experience. To communicate as an authentic leader, you have to look for your own daimon, look into your own experience, and find those themes that are most important to you.

The well of human experience is indeed deep. But the treasures are worth the effort of going into this water, especially if you want to have a conscious and meaningful impact on the world you live in. You don't need to sit in a cave for twenty years; at least some of the treasure is accessible in the context of normal life. Once you discover the themes that matter most to you, you can convert them to inspiration for others—if you are courageous and disciplined enough to do so.

3

Apply Courage and Discipline

Early in 1998, I was introduced to Ed Jensen, soon to retire as chairman of Visa International. Ed was completing a sterling career in financial services and was planning to move and reshape his work life into more humanitarian endeavors.

We met for drinks at the Huntington Hotel in San Francisco to discuss his plans for retirement and explore ways we might work together. He was interested in the whole idea of authentic leadership, given that volunteers are much more challenging to lead than are people who depend on you for a paycheck. Volunteers work for meaning, not for money. The question of how to inspire that kind of loyalty was an important one for Ed.

We spoke about authentic communication and—after some discussion of the difficulty of applying it in a business context—we agreed that the best source of this kind of communication is poetry. With few exceptions, poets write because they have something to say, not because there is a market for it, and because of that motivation, their writing generally touches us in ways that other writing does not.

Ed said that he had written some poetry in secondary school and college, but that he had not written that way in years. He then told me a story.

His father had died a few months before our meeting, and Ed sorted through the attic at the family house. He had come across a folder with letters in it, and began to read the first one casually. He saw that it was an essay . . . a letter of acknowledgment to his parents for their sacrifice and love. He was into the second page before he realized that he was the author; he had written it as part of some final assignments in college.

"I could never write that essay today," he said. "Everything I write now sounds like a memo."

My mind went to my own bookshelves and writings, as I reflected on the number of times I had expressed this same frustration in my own longing and search for authenticity. After our conversation, I sent Ed a poem of Derek Walcott's, reprinted here with permission.

Love After Love

The time will come
when, with elation,
you will greet yourself arriving
at your own door, in your own mirror,
and each will smile at the other's welcome,

and say, sit here. Eat.
You will love again the stranger who was your self.
Give wine. Give bread. Give back your heart
to itself, to the stranger who has loved you

all your life, whom you ignored
for another, who knows you by heart.
Take down the love letters from the bookshelf,

the photographs, the desperate notes,
peel your own image from the mirror.
Sit. Feast on your life.[1]

Ed sent me a note by return e-mail: "Thank you for sending the poem about me."

While I haven't seen Ed since, I do know that he went on to work most effectively in the field of economic development in impoverished areas, and is inspiring others with his work and his communication to this day. I also know what a gift he gave me with this one sin-gle observation.

Finding Your Voice: The Courage to Take a Stand

At some time in our lives, usually at a very young age, most of us abandon our real voice and adopt a more conventional one, in the legitimate desire to communicate in an acceptable way. Unfortunately, that altered voice can take over completely. Suddenly twenty years have gone by and we have missed many opportunities to use our real voice, the one that belongs to that "stranger" who has loved us all of our lives and whom we ignored for another. Fortunately, that neglected voice has real power, and will generally come out whether we like it or not.

In 1980, I was running a fairly large sales operation for IBM on the West Coast of the United States. My fifteen-year career with the company had been studded with success, but I had made a lifestyle deci-sion to move back to the West Coast in the mid-1970s, and didn't intend to move east again. Accordingly, my interest in my job had been waning. I was ready to leave, and I was being helped along by the growing bureaucracy of the firm.

At that time, all companies doing interstate commerce were re-quired by the federal government to compile extensive reports on the status of their Equal Opportunity efforts. Unfortunately, this onerous reporting requirement had soured most managers, and the bureau-cratic process had received far more attention than the real work of hiring and promoting minorities. In January of that year, a well-meaning human resources vice president had instituted yet one more layer of reporting, requiring all managers to have written develop-ment plans on file for each person in their organization who was in an "affected class," essentially women and minorities. This require-ment spawned an exercise in filling out forms rather than stimulating any real extra effort at authentic career counseling and develop-ment. Those managers already doing the job of developing their peo-ple merely had an extra burden.

Each quarter, the nine of us responsible for our division's national results reviewed our progress with senior management in New Jersey. At the third-quarter review that year, the vice president who had instituted the development plan requirement entered the meeting and asked us what we thought of it. He was obviously looking for agreement. I heard a voice say, "I think it is the biggest bunch of B.S. I've ever seen." It was a full five seconds before I realized that it had been my voice uttering these words. Clearly my career was in serious jeopardy, and in the following mini-seconds that seemed like hours, I knew that I didn't care.

The next voice, after a stunned silence, was that of my boss and mentor, Ed Mosner. "I couldn't agree with you more," he said. "How would you like to fix it?"

Most people have experienced some moment similar to this, either vicariously or personally. Finding one's voice is not the same as discovering values, but often in that moment of frustration when values are violated, the voice can't be stopped. Popeye, the sailor cartoon character of the 1950s and 1960s, was known for such moments of frustration. He was patient to a point, but when pushed to the wall by his cartoon rival, or when his friend and lover Olive Oyl was threatened, he would raise his right index finger high, puff his cheeks and mutter, "That's all I can stands, I can't stands no more!" Out would come a can of spinach; he would down it in one swallow and proceed to take care of the situation, usually with physical force.

Such moments of expression are mythic, in that they signal a "coming of age," a willingness to "stand" for something. In movies, as in real life, these moments can often inspire us, as people throw their lives (or as in my case, their careers) into the flame of conviction about an issue. Whether it is Todd Anderson (in the movie *Dead Poet's Society*) standing on his desk to defend his teacher, Mr. Keating, or an impassioned "Braveheart" sounding a battle cry for Scotland, the meaning is clear . . . some things are worth speaking out for, even worth dying for. And money, prestige, and safety cannot stand in their way.

Because Ed Mosner valued authenticity over politics, his response to my outburst was positive. I might not have been so fortunate. Many are not. Yet people who take stands based upon their beliefs have moved closer to leadership. They are clear about what matters, and they have mustered the courage to speak in defense of that value.

But being impetuous is not leading. I could hardly claim that my outburst about the development plan inspired anyone. Horrified, yes. Inspired, no. Ed's act of grace extended my career by two years, and I did indeed get involved in emphasizing the "doing" part of development over the "reporting" part of development. But as I began the task of turning the bureaucratic process into some meaningful result, I realized I had to communicate about it in a different way. Ranting and raving weren't going to work. Many people were emotionally invested in the process in place, and most were skeptical of making any change at all. I would have to have a disciplined and inclusive approach to get anyone's attention, and my communication would have to reflect something far greater than merely changing a reporting procedure if I were to inspire others to act.

It wasn't hard to discover that the value that had been violated by this suggested practice was authenticity. In this case, the leaders of my division of IBM had been unconsciously promoting form over substance, letting convention get in the way of actually making a difference. . . . We had been going through the motions. My basic change message had to be supported by the flaw in that motivation and my commitment to change it. The message had to be clear and deep, and it had to be crafted before I could begin to deliver it.

I created my message platform by writing about the strength of my own feeling about authenticity, and about the value of providing equal opportunity as a fundamental right of being an American. My trips to the Jefferson Memorial started to have real meaning in a context other than my own life. As I will describe in Chapter Five, these values had the power to connect me with others, pulling them into the issue on the basis of values, not dwelling on whether the current system was right or wrong, only focusing on what could change to make it better.

The requirement for the development plans stayed in place, but the spirit of completing them changed, and the enforcement of the practice took on a completely different tone. A few years later, the federal government dropped the requirement for extensive reporting. Although I had left IBM long before, I was sure that the managers who were involved in this change were still doing the right thing for the right reason—not just filling out forms.

Only by disciplining your voice can you allow real leadership to emerge. It isn't necessary to wait for your voice to assert itself without your help. In fact, as I can attest, it's better not to wait for that Popeye moment. Better to decide what your values compel you to change and then start writing.

Disciplining Your Voice for Clarity by Writing

To be converted into action, the insights of reflection require the discipline of writing. Authentic as off-the-cuff conversations can be, they often relay only a momentary emotional impulse. For example, we have all heard public speakers who can light a fire in an audience. When such a speaker is finished, everyone in the room wants to do *something*, but no one knows what to do. This same eruptive kind of communication takes place in informal meetings in offices around the world and many of us scramble to comply. Practitioners garner nicknames that portray their style—Old Ironsides, or Neutron Jack.

Communication that moves others to committed action includes both passion and reason. Both are necessary to generate trust and action from others, so that the mind is as fully engaged as the heart. Accordingly, writing is imperative to communicating authentically.

Writing reveals fuzzy thinking, exposes slurred distinctions: it clarifies. That's why it is so difficult. And it takes time, more time to write than to make a few notes. I'm not suggesting that you must sit by a fire and compose with a quill pen. I *am* suggesting that you must compose the *content* of your conviction about what needs to change, even if the words are put to paper by someone else. You must edit such drafts from your own conviction, maintaining your independence from any professional. Writing your own conviction is like Woody Allen's characterization of taking a metaphysics final in college. You can't cheat by looking into the soul of the kid next to you.

Advisers can be very effective, but they have to be chosen carefully. The very best are not just good writers, they are also strong thinkers and coaches who push you to articulate your own thoughts and feelings in the most effective way. Ted Sorenson, John Kennedy's speechwriter, was also Kennedy's chief of staff and conversed with the president every day. By contrast, many of today's communication professionals, excellent as they are as composers, frequently have little access to their principal. They may be able to predict the formal position, but they know little of the inside drive or conviction of the person for whom they write. The people you choose should be trusted associates you respect for more than their technical talent. They should also be willing to ask questions, offer substantive advice, listen and then reflect your own beliefs back to you in language that feels right to you, not only to them.

Even though Mario Cuomo is a superb writer, he includes other associates in his process of constructing messages. In writing his remarks on abortion rights for the Department of Theology at the University of Notre Dame, he relied on two of his staff, both "gifted thinkers and writers, both of them profoundly Catholic and just as troubled as I was by the task of agonizing over the powerful, almost paralyzing issues raised by the abortion question. We wrote, discussed, debated, and finally decided."[2]

Any leadership message you construct will be the basis for most communication you have about your plan to change things for the better. Others can help, but finally, it is your own values, your own commitment to an issue that will determine the power of the message to you, and therefore to others. Whatever response you want from others must happen in you first. Accordingly you must eventually hold the pen yourself, and enlist only helpers who can assist you in drawing out your own conviction.

In Chapters Six through Ten I will discuss, in detail, the components of each section of an effective foundation message and the material that can best move you toward conveying both competence and connection. But as you enter that process, it remains true that reflection, writing, and including the elements of a framework will only provide the *vehicle* for real self-expression. Following the instructions does not *guarantee* authenticity, it only makes it possible. The discipline presented here is like musical notation. It has form and can evoke beauty, but the real *meaning* of any musical performance can only be brought forth by the musician.

A few years ago, Robert Commanday, then music critic for the *San Francisco Chronicle*, illustrated this principle in a critique of a young Russian violinist, Vadim Repin, who had played Tchaikovsky's "Violin Concerto in D Major" with the San Francisco Symphony Orchestra. I had been in the audience, and as a former violinist, I found Repin's technique flawless. He was fast and precise, and drew a standing ovation. But I had noticed only a few phrases of the music where the distinction between the instrument, the violinist, the orchestra, and the music disappeared. As it turned out, those moments were also noticed by the critic and used as a contrast with the rest of the performance.

Commanday's critique read, in part, as follows (emphasis mine):

> Repin has a grand, exceptionally big, warm tone, a phenomenal technique that commanded this concerto, even challenging the finale to go as vivacissimo as the orchestra can play it. *Hiding somewhere underneath that there must be a personality, a musician with something to say of his own.* . . . He played most of the first movement cadenza as if smoothness in bowing . . . were the principal expressive idea. [But] after the cadenza, Repin began to set off and reveal the phrases.
>
> The Finale was a rouser, faster and faster, keener and keener, and the audience loved it. [But], the *musicality must develop alongside the technique and purely violinistic mastery and*

*be there the whole way . . . yes . . . at 21, the essential matter is
not just how he plays but why.*[3]

A master violinist's reading and playing of a musical score does
not ensure *his self-expression* through the instrument. And your writing a change message in full does not ensure the emergence of your
authentic voice.

Musical notation and words only *represent* the real thing. After
you have written your convictions, you must communicate them
from the inside out, bringing your own internal voice to the symbols
on the page.

Authentic communication is a continual dance between the
heart and the mind, and between you and those with whom you
communicate. Your own engagement in the subject will provide a
mirror of what you are engendering in others. As you are passionate,
convinced, and committed about the change you want to make, so
others can become passionate, convinced, and committed as they
engage with you around your message.

Before you go public, your message needs your life, not merely
your ideas. The words you use and the way you relate them will determine whether you will be perceived as a leader or merely as a person with a lot of passion around a good idea, whether you want to lead
or merely to get results. Once your passion is clear and your message
concise, you need to make a conscious decision to lead, not merely
to express yourself. In that decision to lead, you will be committing
yourself to understand more about the way you relate—and the way
others receive it.

4

Decide to Lead

The first two principles, *discovering what matters* and *applying courage and discipline*, yield insight into values and the practical changes that you think need to be implemented. Yet the discovery of values and the disciplining of the voice through writing do not, in themselves, create leadership behavior. Rather than leading, you could decide to become an artist or author, an invaluable individual contributor who achieves outstanding results alone. Each of us can do exceptional work that expresses our values yet rarely communicate with anyone else directly. Even when we do communicate, we can merely tell people what we need to accomplish our own ends. Many philosophers contribute in this way, as do many of our most accomplished and popular psychologists, many of our best business and political consultants, and many of our best thinkers. Important work—but it is not the same as leading.

Leading is a personal pursuit that by definition *involves* other people. The primary distinction between a leader and someone who merely conceives and expresses good ideas or examples, or one who merely gets results, is the ability to relate to others. And although the logical mind is a great tool for gaining agreement, it is not sufficient to build relationship.

Leadership Built on Emotional Intelligence

Since 1995, Daniel Goleman and others have made the case for emotional intelligence (EI) as the basis for the kind of leadership that engages others to commitment.

The idea of EI seems intuitively correct; few of us make the really important decisions in life based on logic alone, and those who do live with emotional regret. Goleman and others have shown us the science-based brain research that makes the importance of emotional intelligence credible, if not incontrovertible.

The conclusion of that research is that any decision to lead rather than to merely contribute to the body of knowledge, or to merely achieve results, has to include a commitment to learn about and enhance, through practice, our emotional breadth as well as our ability to relate to others' emotions. Because relationships are forged through communication, we have to also become skilled in emotional communication, to know not only when and how to reveal our own emotions but also when and how to acknowledge those of the people we want to lead.

Thanks to this work, the ability to emotionally connect is now widely recognized as a core competence of leading. What hasn't been recognized as much is the hard work it takes to relate authentically, to do more than merely go through the motions. What Goleman calls "resonance" is not just being on the same page intellectually, it is being in the same zone emotionally, sharing the same dreams, hoping for the same outcomes, sharing the feelings of risk, communicating about joy, fear, hope, and frustration.

To block emotions so that we don't feel them is pathological; to ignore them or to treat them as unimportant is to minimize the primary drivers of our actions and deaden our ability to relate to others. As with understanding our values, developing emotional intelligence starts with the ability to discern the emotions on our own internal landscape. Without this basic ability, we cannot move on to the other, more subtle elements, adjusting our emotional responses and developing empathy, the ability to recognize, acknowledge, and respond to emotions in others.

Giving Voice to Emotions

Nowhere is this skill more demonstrable than in our personal relationships. When I was divorced in 1982, I was fortunate to be awarded full physical custody of my two sons, even as my five-year-old daughter was leaving to live with her mom. The boys were thirteen and eleven at the time, and over the next few years, we three learned the importance of being emotionally honest together. I can remember vividly one of my sons packing his things in his room and telling me that he was moving out, either to go live with a friend or to go to his mom's house some fifty miles away. The disagreement between us had been over something substantive, and I realized, given his strong will, that he would probably go, and would never be able to return, even if it were the obvious and right thing to do. As he stood there with a small bag packed, a part of me wanted to send him on his way and tell him that he would regret it. But as emotion welled up in me, as the possibility of his leaving became real, I was able to tell him that although we had had a disagreement, and we would have to work it out, I really didn't want him to leave. I told him that I loved him, and that despite still being angry, I was also afraid that we were doing the wrong thing. I did not want to lose my special connection with him. He stayed, actually admitting that he didn't want to lose the connection either. This was not the only "learning opportunity." Through a series of interactions such as this one, all three of us learned and began to appreciate the importance of giving voice to our emotions.

This act of making an internal conversation external has made it possible to defuse many disagreements over time, and has even healed old wounds. Judith Honesty, a colleague at BlessingWhite, calls this process "showing the math." Those who took mathematics from good teachers know the accuracy of the metaphor. By showing our actual work in a problem rather than just the answer, we earned partial credit for our efforts even if we did not get the right solution to the problem. In the same way, by revealing that inside emotional conversation, or the *process* of "getting the answer" about other problems, we earn partial credit, or credibility, from the listener, even if we are awkward in expressing it, or even if they think we have the wrong answer.

Years later, this willingness and ability to "show the math" made it possible to reconcile with my daughter, who had been distant, had perhaps felt left out, and who had naturally been influenced by being essentially separate. She and I had one pivotal conversation at a restaurant in a small California town where we both stopped pretending not to be hurt, and "showed the math." After nearly twenty years of being cordial with one another, real love had a place to show up. And it did.

What does this have to do with leadership? Everything.

In the mid-1990s, I was coaching a top-level executive who had as much potential as anyone I had met. His track record of getting results was sterling; it included assuming responsibility for three very large operations in three very large companies, all within a seven-year period. He had international experience and an advanced degree from a prestigious university. He was one of the smartest, quickest people I had encountered.

He also had one of the highest needs of anyone I had met to satisfy an enormous ego.

Unfortunately, his communication reflected his hubris. The only emotions he could express at work were frustration, impatience, and anger. Rather than acknowledging these as signs of his own drive to succeed that might need modification as he gained responsibility, he spewed them out indiscriminately in increasingly heavy doses to those who worked for him. At the zenith of his career, he was responsible for nearly 70 percent of the operations and 80 percent of the people in the company. His default was to engender fear, not hope; insecurity, not confidence.

In the short term, his group got excellent results. They exceeded even the most optimistic forecasts of the strategists.

In the wake of his short-term success, he was hoping to be promoted to run the company, and as a step toward that possibility, asked for some feedback on his ability to lead. A colleague administered a 360-degree feedback instrument to his direct reports. The results were predictable. While our executive was at the top of the "competence" ranking, he was at the bottom of the "connection" ranking. His style of communicating not only engendered fear in those who encountered him, it also demoralized many of his charges.

In the debrief of the responses to the instrument, the executive asked the right question: "Do I have to change to be successful?" My colleague and I replied almost simultaneously, "No, unless you want to stay here." He did not change. Instead, he left under duress shortly thereafter, totally unable to leverage his ability to hold people accountable because of his inability to engender trust.

He went on to start another enterprise that skyrocketed in the beginning and died when it needed energy from others to continue to grow.

This profile is not unusual for turnaround specialists in sports, business, or politics. When operations are in disarray, intimidation from a strict no-nonsense autocrat can indeed turn people's attention sharply to their responsibilities. But this sharp attention to accountability isn't enough to sustain success for the long term. Only in recognizing and acknowledging our own feelings can we recognize and acknowledge others'. And only then can a leader develop the bond of trust necessary for commitment and continued contribution.

Managing Your Emotional Response

Strong feelings are of course common, even essential, in the world of leading change. If leaders recognize their own automatic emotional responses, they can actually adjust their communication to be more appropriate, less damaging, more inspiring.

Dave Pottruck, friend, client, and CEO of The Charles Schwab Corporation, reported an example of the need for emotional intelligence in Clicks and Mortar.

Earlier in 1999, I spoke to a conference of Wall Street analysts interested in the financial services industry. The speaker just before me in the program was an analyst with an expertise in electronic commerce. He commented during his remarks that the competition for electronic commerce in our industry was essentially over, that the discount brokerages had won, and that the banks were "losers." I was the next speaker, and as I promised my host, I spoke about Schwab's expansion on the Internet as well as some recent new business ventures that we had tried, including clearing mutual fund transactions for third parties and offering term life insurance. During the question and answer period that followed, one participant asked me if "Schwab would become a bank." I immediately quipped, "Why would we want to become a loser?"

Now, I made the remark as a joke, and it did get a laugh, but even as it was coming out of my mouth, I was picturing it as a headline, printed by a reporter who was in the room. I went on to answer the question more completely, and after the session, found the reporter. I told him that I realized how my "witty comment" would look quoted out of context, and that I clearly shouldn't have made the comment. He was gracious, said that he understood, and did not print the quip. But in the interchange and in my own reminder to myself, I learned again the care with which a leader has to comport himself.[1]

What Dave did not report in his account was a later conversation he had with the communications group at Schwab. The chief communication officer was trying to explain the lesson to the group: "Watch what you say in front of reporters." Dave added the following comment: "Yes," he said, "it is certainly important to watch what we say in front of reporters, but the real reason I shouldn't have made that comment has nothing to do with the press. I shouldn't have made that comment because anyone who heard me refer to someone else or some group as 'losers' would assume I was capable of saying that about them when they were not listening. It is a lesson for me to look at to build my own character. If I feel that way, I need to be aware of it, so that I can manage that response in myself and build my own character."

Dave's response shows the link between empathy and character that Goleman and others refer to:

> There is growing evidence that fundamental ethical stances in life stem from underlying emotional capacities. . . . For one, impulse is the medium of emotion; the seed of all impulse is a feeling bursting to express itself in action. Those at the mercy of impulse . . . who lack self-control . . . suffer a moral deficiency. The ability to control impulse is the base of will and character. By the same token, the root of altruism lies in empathy, the ability to read emotions in others; lacking a sense of another's need or despair, there is no caring.[2]

Certainly, any who saw the 2002 testimony of Enron executives before the U.S. Congress saw a dearth of emotional expression from these apparently intelligent men and women, similar to the response we saw in 1998 with the testimony of the tobacco executives who all stood and affirmed that they did not believe that smoking cigarettes caused cancer. These outwardly unfeeling, uncaring "leaders" were not only bereft of much self-knowledge, they were apparently empty of empathy. Few showed any remorse, much less any responsibility. It would be easy to conclude that they were short on character as well.

Becoming Aware and Wary of Self-Importance

Understanding our own emotions and developing empathy toward others also exposes our own egos and need for recognition.

Jim Collins's research on leadership that brought companies from "good to great" emphasizes this aspect of leadership. He says, "Leadership is about creating a climate where the truth is heard and the brutal facts confronted. There's a huge difference between the opportunity to 'have your say' and the opportunity to be heard. The good-to-great leaders understood this distinction, creating a culture wherein people had a tremendous opportunity to be heard and, ultimately, for the truth to be heard."[3]

Being able to create this kind of climate requires a high degree of emotional intelligence and a willingness to give up the controlling role in the organization, choosing instead to lead.

In the year 2000, Tom Murphy was chief information officer of Royal Caribbean Cruises Ltd. in Miami, Florida. He had enjoyed a meteoric career and had jumped from job to job fixing troubled organizations. He came to RCCL in 1999 after successful stints at Marriott and Omni Hotels, where he had been the youngest officer at both companies. In these and other organizations, he had quickly turned bad situations around and then left for another opportunity.

He started at RCCL in the same way. He rapidly assessed the IT team, reorganized, and began to get results. They won Department of the Year in 1999, consecutive Best Places to Work in IT awards in 2000 and 2001, and multiple honors for Innovation and Web Excellence.

Unlike many turnaround specialists, Tom was not an emotional cripple. He had a gregarious personality, and he approached his job with passion and commitment to exceeding customer expectations. But as he later realized, the focus was always on him. In early 2001, he partnered with his organizational specialist to get the team some leadership training. I met him at the first session of an executive course in values clarification, leadership, and culture building in the Miami offices of the company.

Because the course is designed to bring a team together around some principles, maximizing its benefit requires a great deal of emotional intelligence from the participants. They are asked to be vulnerable, and also to hold each other accountable for honest communication about problems in the organization.

Tom demonstrated a quick wit and with it a sharp tongue, and yet had the capacity to goad others on to greater participation than they would have otherwise been capable of. I liked him immensely and felt that he had substantial talent and energy. At the same time, I noticed that although he managed to maintain the intellectual respect of the group, he stayed on the outside, not really engaging personally.

This is what Tom told me about the effect of his experience in the training:

> My style, called a lightning rod or "Organizational Identifi-cation" by Harvard's Abraham Zaleznik, helped IT to over-come strong negative perceptions on the part of the business and strong internal challenges from early on. There is power in getting people to identify with you so strongly that you be-come a constant presence in their thinking. When you become an object of identification to your team, when you allow them to use you like that, the result is enormous cohesion. . . . There is a contagious power to this identification and it creates a singular focus throughout the organization.
>
> What I didn't realize at the time was that this approach has unseen ramifications that can negatively impact the leader-ship team, management group and IT's overall performance over time. If the group becomes overly reliant on a single source for energy, passion and vision, where does it go when that source is no longer available? . . . My history of moving from job to job was well known and . . . I felt a sort of perverse sense of pride that came when a former organization started to falter after I had left.

As a result of this realization, Tom made a decision to stay at RCCL and work to develop the people who worked with him. In making that commitment to his team, he was able to become more authentic in his communication, and, in his words, "discuss issues that we would not have otherwise discussed." "As we started deal-ing with one another on a different level, our trust grew," said Tom. "We were drawn closer to each other at a personal level as well." It was by exercising emotional intelligence that he made a major step forward in leadership.

From Being the Boss to Becoming a Leader

Good leaders get people to work for them. Great leaders get people to work for a cause that is greater than any of them—and then for one another in service of that cause. By shifting the focus of his leadership, adopting the practice of introspection and authenticity, Tom has delivered more than results. He has delivered a group of people who want to struggle together to accomplish something none could do alone.

This is emotional intelligence: knowing about emotions, recognizing them in yourself, being appropriately vulnerable, and relating, or resonating, with others.

We come to this learning individually and, as I've discovered, sometimes with great effort. Some people learn earlier than others, usually because their crucible is hotter, their experience more intense.

In 2000, I met Joe DeCola, a producer of *The Today Show* at NBC. I thought the meeting was about some potential book publicity, but it turned out to be about my own education. As we chatted about the attributes of authenticity, Joe told me of his eighteen-year-old daughter, Rebecca. She was going to be a freshman at Oberlin, and had graduated from the Buxton School, a small private high school in Williamstown, Massachusetts. It was the brilliantly conceived ritual of the school to have each graduating senior give a short talk at graduation about what had informed their lives.

I should fill in some context. Joe and his former wife were very active in the political movements of the 1960s, separated in the 1980s when Rebecca was young, and kept a healthy relationship in her parenting. That's no small feat for any couple, but they managed all this even as Joe began to openly identify himself as homosexual.

He was clearly proud of Rebecca's graduation speech. I asked him for a copy, almost as an afterthought, and he obliged. With my first reading, I laid it on my desk as tears welled up. I include the full text here, as a premier example of the growing of emotional intelligence and the impact of that growth on the way in which one person relates to others who may or may not agree with them. It is reprinted with Rebecca's permission:

> When I was small, I got to be in marches. I marched for abortion rights, equal rights for women, gay pride, AIDS funding. I went to folk concerts with my mother to raise money for the hungry, I worked at shelters to give soup to the homeless and I got to throw pink glittery Fairy Dust at angry people who said that my father and Adam and Steve would all burn in Hell.
>
> When I was a little larger, I was part of an environmental action committee and yelled about Styrofoam and recycling. I collected books, clothes, canned foods for people in Rwanda, New York and Kosovo. I volunteered over the summer for the Mohawk, and worked with the mentally ill. I raised money for Mumia and tried my darndest to not support corporate greed. I boycotted the Gap, Domino's, Exxon, Shell, Home Depot. I went hiking a lot, and I know about things like minimum impact and sustainable living. I have farmed with organic self-sufficient farmers, driven an efficient car across the country, and written letters protesting against logging, sweatshops, apartheid, hate crimes, prison systems, toxin dumping, the death penalty, and commercial fish trolling.
>
> These actions are important. They are valid and valiant and real. They are also part of being a little kid and being able to say that Barbies are bad for women, and your parents are Democrats, and you wear purple so you're okay. They made me feel aware, empowered, and moral. They made up a set of understandings which fit comfortably into a liberal sense of self. I do not have this sense anymore. I still think that there are some things that are just simply good, or simply unjust, but the list is getting increasingly smaller. The issues are much more blurred, the questions far too large for me to answer. I have realized recently that it is more and more difficult to make any STATEMENTS.

I take much longer pauses before I say things and there are fewer and fewer T-shirts that express what I am trying to say.

I have come into a sense of my own ignorance and naïveté, which is both exciting and paralyzing. On one hand, it means that I want to learn more. I want to become more educated, and in doing this I will be able to affect things truly powerfully and precisely.

On the other hand, it means I have lost the ability to just act. To directly confront things in that romantic raging way I thought I always could. I am more cautious, more fearful. I feel less sure of myself, and in losing the sense that there is some immutable solid truth out there, I lose my sense of when and how to act.

Simply, the world is a complex, confusing place. It has taken me eighteen years to realize this in some of its entirety. I am trying to reconcile this understanding with the fact that I want to engage. I am trying to define my place in all of it. I don't want to simplify my life; I don't want to follow some guru's ten easy steps to happiness. I want to eat cheese and be honest. I don't want to be lost in idealistic adoration for this or that cause or this or that righteous leader, but I also don't want to throw my hands up and see everything with the grownup club's discussing-the-ills-of-the-world-over-latte distance. I want to really know what I am talking about before I start yelling.

Building this emotionally intelligent aspect of communication into your fundamental message will shift your good idea to a foundation for your inspirational interaction with others. The decision to lead has to include a decision to get to know your emotional makeup, recognize and respect emotions when they arise, communicate them responsibly, and develop the empathy necessary to relate to others on this same plane.

The upcoming section will introduce ways to build some of this capability into your message.

PART TWO

The Leadership Message

Connected and Complete

To win followers, leaders must transfer more than information. They must also transmit what they see and feel so that others see and feel it. I've used the terms *transfer* and *transmit* purposely; one is transactional, the other is holistic. "Seeing and feeling" are the subjective bases of your conviction. You have to offer credibility and trustworthiness, confidence and passion, facts and faith. When listeners agree with your story, they see, feel, and understand the need for change. And in an age of discontinuity, an age when the past does not logically predict the future, it is even more critical that you build a substantial emotional bridge between what was and what needs to be.

Few people view issues broadly enough to recognize their importance in relationship to other issues. Most tend to view each change as insular, as not affecting the other multiple aspects of their lives. In speaking about a need for change, you, as a leader, are relating your rendition of the past, present, and future of the issue as well as enlarging others' perspective about the ripple effects of change. You are compelling your constituents to engage with your larger and longer view. This understanding is crucial because different versions of your story will lead to different conclusions and hence to different opinions and feelings about whether change is needed—and if it is, about its nature and optimum timing.

The chapters of Part Two elaborate on ways to connect, to create resonance with other people, and then suggest a framework—or template—for the development of the fundamentals of your message, a platform to stand on for all your leadership communication. The framework will guide you in developing a message that will resonate with you, the leader, and that will form the basis for all your interactions with others—speeches, discussions, written communications, and conversations—about the change you want to effect in the world. The elements of the framework are establishing competence and building trust, creating shared context, declaring and describing a compelling future, and committing to action.

Consider this framework as a "questioning machine" for your use. If you have asked yourself the questions implied by the framework elements and explicit in this book, and if you have answered these questions authentically, then your message will come through with passion and conviction. People will resonate with it.

Not every communication opportunity will require you to discuss every element of the framework. But working through the framework first will enable you to put the necessary elements in place. In the process, you will increase your own clarity and deepen your conviction: you will be inspired to move ahead with the changes that are important to you.

5

Connect with Others

Rebecca DeCola, whose graduation speech formed the conclusion to Chapter Four, was, at eighteen, coming to terms with her need to relate to others in new and different ways—not to always oppose, not to ever appease, but to consider knowledge that might not be simple and relationships that are formed from complexity. How she pursues that exploration and applies what she learns will determine her ability to connect with others, to engage with them to find and create progress. Her success hinges on how she views several questions:

- What causes us to be attracted or repelled by others before they have given any outward signals that would indicate friend or foe?

- Why do we have an affinity for some people even if we disagree with them?

- What is the initial basis for trust?

- How do human beings who don't speak the same language connect?

- What are the implications for leadership, for communicating about change?

New research on the human brain and its function as mediator and guardian shows us new possibilities. While the reptilian stem of our brains gives us impulses to fight or flee, and the cortex reasons and decides, the workhorse of the system, the limbic brain, is receiving and interpreting data from conscious and unconscious systems and routing it to the appropriate place.

Unspoken Harmonies

This marvelous arbiter of sensations operates at a rate that is roughly eighty thousand times as fast as the cerebral cortex, processing up to 10 million bits of input per second. It reads the input from the senses and decides what to send to the cortex for expanded awareness, decision, and action. It processes images, sounds, and other subtle sensory information, sends signals to the appropriate glands, and then monitors the emotions. This most interesting capability of the limbic brain gives us the ability to make unconscious judgments about the trustworthiness of others, and perhaps even allows us to sense the meaning behind activities that are going on around us. Through this system, we get into synch with other human beings, a capability referred to as "limbic resonance."[1]

Simply put, limbic resonance is what we call "connection," the magic sense of another's state, whether it is signaled by feelings of dread or feelings of mutual attraction. It is this resonance that makes our experience of someone else a deeper experience than merely seeing two biologically similar eyes. In their marvelous work on the physiology of love, Thomas Lewis and his collaborators testify: "To the animals capable of bridging the gap between minds, limbic resonance supplies the wordless harmony we see everywhere but take for granted—between mother and infant, between a boy and his dog, between lovers holding hands across a restaurant table. . . ."[2]

And, I would add, between leaders and those they inspire.

As we begin to develop our message, then, we need to look at the specific ways of communicating that appeal to the limbic brain, to that part of our brain that doesn't make distinctions or judgments but rather connects with the other holistically. That part of our brain relates to image, story, and experience.

Creating Images That Resonate

It's true: A picture *is* worth a thousand words. Images are retained in our consciousness in vivid detail; when we recall them, often it is with the emotion originally associated with the image. In contrast, words and concepts are retained as mere ideas unless they can hook into emotional experience.

The most used data suggests that people are apt to retain roughly 80 percent of what they see and only 20 percent of what they hear. This knowledge has sold millions of overhead projectors and even more copies of PowerPoint. Wonderful as these products are for display—and for allaying the fear of exposure and personal vulnerability—they remove presenters from audiences and discourage real contact. The images that we most vividly recall are not those from clip art, or from the reflection of complex material on a screen. Rather, the images we remember are those we can see in a greater context of life, those created by human communication.

William Blake's words, "to see a universe in a grain of sand and eternity in an hour," accurately describe the perspective of the effective leader. What we see and feel in one dimension can be translated to others through our imagination—our *ability to image*. Thoughtful leadership communication includes memorable images, images bolstered by analogy and metaphor.

Connecting the Known and the Unknown with Analogies

Metaphor means to "carry across." Analogy and metaphor carry us from a known to an unknown, or from the subjective to the objective. Is the building of the information superhighway in the 1990s like the building of the automotive highway system in the 1950s? Is cutting corporate costs to avoid layoffs like cutting family costs to avoid having college students come home for lack of tuition? Is creating a national health care system analogous to creating the social security system? Is love a flower, a bird, or a pothole? Was the feeling you had at sunset yesterday like seeing a sudden opening in a violent storm?

The answers to these questions will bring others to a realization of the unknown from a reminder of the known, or an emotional understanding of the nature of a subjective feeling.

The issues of value and meaning that appear in our personal lives can also be universalized. The leader knows that the longings and the values of people do not change with the area of application and that most people want to find deep meaning in their work. Indeed, as Margaret Wheatley observed, "Most people want their work to serve a greater good, to help other people. But we seldom pause and reconnect with the initial idealism and desire to serve that led us into our professions."[3] This is not news, but somehow too many of us forget the importance of it in the humdrum sound of life. We long to be committed at work and to express our values in our community. Unfortunately, many feel constrained to do so, afraid of the penalty of being incorrect or convinced that their sincerity will meet with the stiff resistance of a bureaucracy. Skilled leaders communicate that, with regard to values and meaning, every situation can be seen as analogous to all others. Leaders who have mastered a metaphorical view of the world can infuse their principles with images, instilling a sense of possibility in the imagination of their listeners.

The implication of metaphorical communication is that the unknown future of the change you are advocating will be essentially the same as the known outcome in the analogy. Because change begets some fear, those with whom you communicate will make a *complete* association. Choose your analogy with care, for some of the conclusions might be counterproductive to your cause. For example, food biotechnology experts have drawn analogies between the development of genetically engineered food and the development of the monoclonal antibodies used in modern medicine. While the process is similar, few people want to consider food and medicine as equivalent. One executive even commented, "Within the next few years, you will be able to open your refrigerator and your medicine cabinet and see the same thing!" This image was not helpful to his cause.

Effective analogies point others *only* toward a conclusion that is in keeping with your intent. In 1992, NASA Administrator Daniel Goldin addressed the Association of Space Explorers in Washington, D.C., on the question of why the United States should send a human expedition to Mars. In setting the stage for his advocacy, he drew the following analogy from the time of Columbus's voyage:

> Only [Queen] Isabella was willing to look beyond the many problems on her own shores, and see the potential reward for her investment in the future. The voyages of Columbus set the stage for more Spanish explorers, who turned Spain into a great world power. As a consequence, the language and culture of Spain prevail in most of Latin America to this day.
>
> On the other side of the world, however, in China . . . the intended destination of Columbus . . . their emperors turned their back on the rest of the world. Sixty years prior to 1492, Chinese explorers had traveled as far as Africa. But a new emperor considered such journeys wasteful extravagances. His successors burned the boats, and banned all Chinese from leaving the country. Those who tried could be executed.
>
> That 15th-century decision to *not* explore still reverberates in China today. What was one of the world's most advanced and innovative civilizations is today an inward-looking nation. For a country with the most people on Earth, it is almost an afterthought in global affairs.[4]

This is an apt comparison because the conclusions are unmistakable. The nation that has the foresight to explore space will lead progress in other areas as well. If we fail to fund a mission to Mars, someone else will, and our nation will be forever catching up to other nations that demonstrated more courage and foresight.

A leader chooses analogies and metaphors carefully, knowing that the entire organization will feel the impact of the choice. The response is largely a function of the experience of those who hear the analogies and metaphors, whether they are familiar with the shared characteristics, and whether they react positively or negatively to those characteristics. In 2000, Karen Chang, head of branches and business development for Schwab, was addressing five hundred of her charges regarding their need to provide more specific customer solutions. Karen is one of the most respected women in American business—and, in my view, also among the best-dressed. She came up with the following to make her point that her organization had to be more flexible in meeting individual client needs: "We need to be more like Nordstrom's. One customer can walk in needing an Armani suit, another might want some Donna Karan evening wear, and still another might simply want a Nordstrom's brand T-shirt. They can all be served in the same store." Karen's analogy got the point across in a succinct way, and in a way that a major portion of her audience understood instantly. For those who might not, she continued: "Now I know that some of you guys didn't understand what I just said. You probably think that you saw 'Armani' on the menu at last night's Italian restaurant, and you've never heard of this 'Donna Karan' chick, but I'm tired of sports metaphors!" Very effective; extremely memorable.

Timothy Wirth, now in charge of allocating Ted Turner's environmental fund at the United Nations, used an apt analogy to explain the relationship between the environment and the economy. "Stated in the jargon of the business world," says Wirth, "the economy is a wholly owned subsidiary of the environment. All economic activity is dependent on the environment and its underlying resource base. When the environment is finally forced to file for bankruptcy under Chapter 11 because its resource base has been polluted, degraded, dissipated and irretrievably compromised, then the economy goes down to bankruptcy with it."[5]

The implications are clear. If we don't take care of the environment, the economy will eventually fail. The analogy is consistent, and the conclusions well-illustrated.

Transferring Characteristics Through Metaphor

Whereas analogies lead to a conclusion based on a specific comparison, metaphors create an implied comparison, a picture that can be generalized in the imagination. All attributes of the metaphor are ascribed to the new situation, and conclusions are drawn from that image about how entire systems should behave.

Are the people in your company "human resources" (like other resources of capital or facilities), "team members" (as they are referred to at Target), or "partners" (as they are referred to at Starbucks)? If human beings are referred to as parts of a machine, then they will be seen as discrete entities, will be replaced or repaired when they break down, will be the concern of the "maintenance manager," and will become obsolete when more modern or less expensive parts become available. If these same human beings are *parts of an organism*, they will be seen as integral to the whole, will be considered irreplaceable, will be the concern of every other part of the organism, and will receive preventive care. Since a strong metaphor can determine the mind-set for thinking about an entire system, it can be very powerful indeed.[6]

Metaphor connects as an image, and therefore evokes an emotional response. As a leader communicates the need for change, choosing metaphors becomes central to managing the emotional response of others. Certain images may come naturally to you, generally out of your own experience; others will see you and themselves actually operating in the metaphor.

John Ure, a technology manager at Agilent's Networking Solutions Group in Europe, drew on his interest in music when developing a change message about a broken supply chain process:

> To me, the present situation feels like an orchestra that is full of reasonably competent musicians, but they are not all playing in the same key. Indeed, one or two aren't even playing from the same score. With two business units, there are two orchestras trying to play different bits of Elgar's "Enigma Variations." The Business Unit managers are the conductors. I'm in the orchestra somewhere, probably leading the wind section. You are all in the orchestra, some of you as players, some as section leaders, some of you playing in both orchestras. Lucky you. The audience is the end customer. The Supply Chain is the music from the moment it leaves the writer's pen to the point that the last dying echo diminishes to nothing.

At the moment it is a fairly raucous affair, in danger of falling on deaf ears.

A sophisticated engineering audience heard this metaphor as a powerful part of John's message and used the orchestral theme in images that pointed toward their resolve to integrate this process.

Metaphors needn't be long or complex to be effective. For example, if you want to change your organization to be more proactive and less reactive, you might use one of several metaphors. "We need to get out of our foxholes and get out there and take the hill!" This military metaphor will be literally received. People will see you as the general, and themselves as the troops. You are collectively engaged in a war, where the stakes are "live or die." They will respond emotionally to these images in the way that is appropriate to the metaphor. This metaphor is the equivalent of the familiar Silicon Valley mantra of the late 1990s, "Eat Lunch, or Be Lunch."

As Karen Chang knew well, the sports metaphor is even more common. "The best defense is a good offense." Or "We need to stop just defending our own net and get out there and score some goals!" This metaphor relates the same need as the military metaphor, to be more proactive, but will create different resonance. Rather than as a general, you will be seen by others as a coach and they will see themselves as members of a team. You are collectively playing a game where the stakes are "win or lose." These perceptions are perhaps more positive, which may account for the persistence of sports metaphor in much of our communication about group performance.

Some metaphors are very succinct. Organized crime, budget deficits, and runaway costs are often referred to as "infectious diseases" or "cancers." These are both powerful metaphors, used frequently to emphasize progressive decay and death. Change is often referred to as "the tide" or "the wind," indicating a force that is beyond the listeners' power to control, but within their power to use for their own purposes. People fill in the attributes of the metaphor and assign them to the subject of discussion without further elaboration. Metaphors of few words create concrete images and make the abstract take form in the real world. Themes such as "climbing mountains" or "crossing chasms" can be used for multiple images and multiple connections.

Richard Mahoney, chairman and CEO of Monsanto, spoke about innovation to the Council on Foreign Relations in 1993 with these images: "Our freedom to innovate is being starved by tax and investment policies that eat our seed corn . . . rather than save it for planting." This has substantially more impact than the abstract translation of the facts: "Our freedom to innovate is being thwarted by policies that consume our investment capital."[7]

And again from Tim Wirth: "This depletion [of the water supply in China] is prompting an exodus from the impoverished interior to the booming coastal cities, which along with the demands of rapid industrialization will combine to form an environmental wall which the Chinese economy will soon hit full-speed." There is hardly a need to explain. Wirth is telling us that the Chinese economic train will be destroyed, everyone on board will be killed, and a recovery will not be made for years. Very effective.

Analogy and metaphor are the first line of image, making concepts into experience and giving the limbic system something with which to resonate. To resonate deeper with an analog understanding of reality, a messenger can use the real thing, the actual occurrence, by telling a story or relating a real personal experience.

The Real World of Narrative

"Tell me a story" is the most repeated refrain in millions of households around the world every night. We want to hear tales of success, of heroes, of tragedy. Hardly anyone says, "Will you read me a few bedtime concepts?" Concepts don't create resonance, but stories do. Leadership communication is about growth and change, words that contain a past, a present, and a future—a story line.

Despite the universal scientific evidence and our collective intuitive sense that time is an illusion, it is, as Einstein said, "a most *stubborn* illusion." The journey through space and time is basic in its import; it is part of the unseen atmosphere of our very existence without regard to culture. The story is to most humans like water is to the fish—so integral to existence that only our self-reflective ability allows us to see it. Everyone's life lies between some version of "once upon a time" and "they all lived happily ever after." Because stories are about our lives, they inspire us with possibility. When leaders build them liberally into communication, others have the opportunity to identify with the story and all its elements—and change it to make the story come true for them as well.

To further my own education as a coach, I occasionally attend programs for therapists on myth and story as methods of healing. In one such program, the director, Jonathan Young, suggested to the therapists that their patients were really looking for editors. "When they come to you," he suggested, "they are saying 'I don't like my story. Can you help me change it?'"

This is actually the task of the leader—to edit the story of the organization, to change the ending, to infuse a new plot line into a story that has become stale and lifeless. It is not merely a matter of adding some people, firing some others, and rearranging the talent. As I will discuss in Chapter Eight, describing a new future is one application of story. But so are inspiring new behavior, building a new culture, and preserving the past. Business literature is rich with stories of great brands: how the FedEx employee hired a helicopter on his own, or the UPS driver found the artist and had a damaged painting repaired for a client in time for Christmas, or the most famous of all, the Nordstrom employee who gave an elderly lady a credit for faulty tires that her former husband had purchased on the Nordstrom site before the store was actually built. Stories will help others actually experience the need for change and the excitement of being part of it. Your message platform has to include stories to ground whatever other evidence you might offer.

Stories as Convincing Evidence

Stories that illustrate the change that is needed, the reason for change, or the effect of change will resonate deeply with others. In fact, stories have been shown to be a most powerful form of evidence.

A study conducted by organizational psychologists Joanne Martin and Melanie Powers concluded that a story provided more credibility to a proposition than a mere declaration by an executive, data alone, or data combined with the same story. In their study, they asserted to four distinct groups of people that a particular company had followed a practice of no layoffs for its entire history. To prove this proposition, they offered one group the data, and to another a simple statement by a senior executive. A third group simply heard a story of a long-term employee, and the fourth got all of the data and heard the story as well. The people in the group that heard only the story were the most convinced.[8] Why would this be the case?

Given current knowledge of the brain, it's reasonable to conclude that the limbic system is the receptor of analog data, like stories, while digital data needs to be processed by the cortex. When presented with digital data, the cortex does what it is supposed to do . . . analyze, doubt, and judge as ways of helping make the correct decision. But analog data like the story does not require judgment or decision. Imagine telling a story around the campfire and hearing someone say, "Oh, I disagree with that!" It doesn't make sense.

Here's an example. I feel very strongly about the value of community, and whenever I am speaking with people about it, advocating a less mobile way of life, I tell this story of my former father-in-law.

Harry was orphaned in the 1920s, when he and his brother were in their early teens. At the time they were living in Seattle, but they had an aunt and uncle in Buffalo. They had a used Model T Ford, and drove the car east from Washington to New York, working when they needed cash to buy food and gasoline. It took them over a month to make the journey.

When they arrived in Buffalo, the boys enrolled in high school. The next year, Harry met Marge. They were married just out of school; Harry went to work for the local bank, and they were able to buy a house in the suburbs. Harry and Marge had a son, and then twin daughters. They joined the local church where Harry served as treasurer, youth group leader, and deacon.

They never moved their home. For the next sixty years, they lived in the same house, raised three well-adjusted children, traveled a little with friends, played cards often, and served in just about every capacity that the community offered. Harry retired from the bank after more than forty years on the job. He died of cancer at home when he was eighty. He was cheerful to the end, and his house was full of friends and family when his spirit left the earth.

While Harry was alive, he was the happiest and most grateful person I knew. Several hundred people attended his funeral. He rarely left Buffalo; he didn't accomplish anything that will be printed in a history book; yet the accolades about his love and devotion to family and community set a benchmark for my own life. His oldest friend present at the funeral had known him for more than seventy years.

There are plenty of data about the delinquency rates of kids who move a lot. There are surveys about the happiness of people who stay in communities for long periods of time. If I were advocating a change in policy that would allow people to remain in their communities, this data would be valuable, but it would not replace the story of Harry Magner. I'm sure that as you read this story, you were relating to it in some way. If you have moved a lot, you might have been reflecting on the consequences. You might have been thinking of parents or friends who have also had the experience of living in one place for a long time. Certainly, you weren't trying to figure out if my numbers were accurate, or wondering about the source of my information.

To most of us, stories are reality; certainly much more so than some concepts or data or a few insights. Using stories to communicate links us with others on a human plane.

Connecting Through Personal Experience

While we relate to stories and place ourselves in metaphor, we absolutely connect with others directly through their personal experience. Metaphor is twice removed, like a copy of a photographic print. Story is once removed, like the negative itself. The personal experience of someone we are directly communicating with is the real thing, not removed at all; and because leadership is personal, the leader's life experience is, without doubt, the best grist for authentic connection.

I can illustrate from my own experience as a speaker. One of my own fundamental values is the freedom and ability to express oneself fully. I'm passionate about this subject, probably as a result of being the smallest kid in my school classes, feeling like I had to speak louder than other kids to be heard. I was also raised on a farm, where each member of the family subjugated his will for the good of the family enterprise. As a final influence, I had an older brother who was substantially larger than I was, and who was occasionally willing to use his size to make sure his little brother didn't become a pest. We had always been close, but his early influence contributed to my later need to be heard. In short, it seemed that few circumstances of my early life encouraged me to speak. Therein lies the source of my passion for self-expression. Accordingly, throughout my corporate and teaching career, I've been a proponent of building skills for developing other people, or, in today's jargon, *empowerment.*

As a result of this passion for self-expression, I have done some analysis of the components of good delegation. While most authorities on this subject correctly identify the objective components of teaching, giving authority and assigning responsibility, few have acknowledged the subjective or emotional components of delegation. Clearly, when real delegation occurs, the boss feels a sense of insecurity, some anxiety that the job will not get done properly—and perhaps also some loss, as the delegation involves letting go of the student, who is no longer connected by the tether of the teaching relationship.

In speaking on this subject, I advocate the use of subjective measurements to confirm that "the boss" has truly empowered someone else. I maintain that if you have taught someone well, then given them complete authority and responsibility, you will feel some anxiety and loss. I offer evidence about this assertion, but also use a personal experience to connect with the authentic experience of the audience. My most profound application of delegation has been as a parent. Since everyone in my audience has been a child, and many of them are currently parents, they inevitably relate to this narrative:

> In 1982 I became a single parent, with sole custody and re-sponsibility for my two sons, then thirteen and eleven years old. For the next few years, we grew uncommonly close through a series of personal trials. I had left my career at IBM and finances had been particularly tight; then I had remarried too hurriedly and had caused some further anxiety. Nonethe-less, they had done well in school and in life, having formed fast friendships and developed solid values. I took tremendous pride (and still do) in their attitude toward life and in the way they conducted themselves.
>
> My oldest son, Jeff, was admitted to the University of Cal-ifornia at San Diego in the fall of 1986, and I elected to drive him to school from San Francisco, a distance of approximately five hundred miles. It was September but still hot in Califor-nia's central valley along Interstate 5. We drove the ten hours making small talk and generally cracking nervous jokes. I tried to be serious about the future a couple of times, but found Jeff only interested in the next months of testing his ability to fend for himself, a very natural concern.
>
> We arrived at the campus in midafternoon and I helped him move into his dorm room, the oldest housing on campus but in a choice location and setting. There was a large square carpet of grass in a quadrangle perimetered by six two-story green buildings. On this particular day, it was sparkling with the nervous laughter of new students and the brilliant colors of Southern California clothes.
>
> Once we got his stuff upstairs and into the room, I started playing "Mr. Mom." I hung pictures, made his bed, and un-packed his Eagle Scout mug. In my concentration I failed to notice the growing contingent of kids in the hall, the escalat-ing sound of music, and the lack of interest on his part in what

I was doing. To his credit, he was very patient, but when his roommate arrived and they began to compare histories, I realized that I had overstayed. We agreed that I would come back that evening to take him to dinner, and I returned to the hotel for a swim. I was beginning to feel anxious.

That evening, just at sunset, I made my way back across the quad to his room. As I approached, I could see the lights of his room and hear the music of the growing gathering of excited newcomers. By now the group was co-ed and there was some dancing in the common area. It was difficult to get his attention as I stood in his room door.

Of course, everything I had done was changed. The beds were on opposite sides of the room, the pictures had been replaced with posters and the Eagle mug was not to be seen. He was engaged in conversation with a group of three students and clearly not pining for an early dinner with his dad.

I finally waved an arm and he joined me in the hall. I suggested that rather than go to dinner he should stay with his friends and that I would see him in the morning for breakfast before I had to return up the coast. He protested just enough, then agreed, letting me know that he was looking forward to breakfast.

I left, and hurried down the stairs and into a nearby grove of eucalyptus trees where I walked alone and cried for about an hour and a half.

This was true delegation. I had done my best to train this young man for the task ahead. I now had to give up any aspect of control over his life and let him live it. My role would be only to respond, not to direct. And because I loved him, it hurt.

I've relayed this experience many times. It never fails to connect me to my own conviction on the subject, and it never fails to connect me with others. Everyone can see themselves in one of the roles in the experience. The feelings that these events engender not only strengthen my advocacy, they also provide a convincing realization that true delegation is difficult; that in the absence of a certain amount of rich and wonderful emotional pain, delegation probably doesn't happen. Because I had this experience and am able to connect it metaphorically with other instances of delegation, I can speak on this subject with a great deal of intensity.

Taking Jeff to college was only one experience. My parents' values, my upbringing, my parents' deaths, my experience on the farm, my successes and failures as an athlete and scholar, my choice of college, my studies, my children's births, my career at IBM, playing music, running across the United States, trips to the old Soviet Union, the times when I have been hurt, elated, sick, married, divorced—these and *all* of the other less notable experiences of my life have formed the convictions that compel me to speak. Fortunately, my biography is not yet over. Experiences that I have today will help form the basis for my conviction in years to come.

So it is with you. Using the relevant experiences of your life to support your advocacy for change is the most effective way of connecting to your own conviction and assuring an authentic bond with others.

The Rules of Engagement

As powerful as stories and experiences are, they are fraught with potential for manipulation. This is all the more reason to be careful as you develop any change message.

Stories can be made up and then generalized illegitimately in an attempt to prove a point. Without data, such generalization is only manipulation. Relating personal experience can also be manipulative and can even substantially detract from a leader's credibility. To others to whom a leader relates, nothing is so clearly inauthentic as an attempt to move them with a disingenuous story or experience. This section offers some guidelines to help avoid these pitfalls.

First, the experience must be clearly relevant to the point you are making. My colleague Harvey Stone likes to refer to the sharing of irrelevant stories as "therapy"—and it certainly has that flavor. If the experience you relate does not support your advocacy, others' response will be a resounding "Huh?"

Second, such experiences must be related from memory, not from a script. When I begin the story of taking Jeff to college, I transport myself through imagination back to the car, back to the central valley of California. With my son in the passenger's seat, I relate what I see and feel during that reverie. I know that the images in my memory will generate a legitimate emotional response in me, and I know that others will respond in a much more holistic way to that actual memory than to a recitation. Consider, would someone you trust *read* you a report of a real incident, or *tell* you his experience of that incident?

At the 1992 U.S. Democratic Convention, vice presidential candidate Albert Gore Jr. told the story of his young son's tragic accident, in which the child was struck by a car and critically injured. During Gore's speech, at precisely the right time, the television cameras cut to the son, now healthy and waving to the crowd from the candidate's box. Gore read the story from the TelePrompTer, and the child received a thunderous ovation.

When Gore's son was first injured, the senator was often interviewed about the impact of the incident on his life and his political career. His answers were always spontaneous, authentic, and touching. Clearly this incident was a turning point in his maturity as a human being. Unfortunately, the version at the convention was cued and rehearsed, and to anyone who had heard the story authentically, its staging at the convention felt like a mere emotional appeal for support. This was calculated personal tone, aimed at manipulating rather than connecting, and to me, it hurt Gore's human credentials. Had he simply left the script and read from his internal memory of the day of the accident, letting the camera operators fend for themselves, he might well have connected with himself again, and therefore with the audience as well.

Gore did this again at the 1998 convention, relating the story of his sister's death from smoking in the same measured tones, for the same dramatic effect. It was a tragic political use of a tragic human event. Did it contribute to a portion of the population's disenchantment with his leadership? I think it did.

The third rule of engagement is to leave nothing out. The memory of a substantive experience includes all aspects of the original happening, the sensory-rich details that guide the imagination of those you are relating to, and bring your own passion to the surface. Exactly what you saw and heard, exactly what you perceived and felt; these minutiae will turn the experience into one that taps your own heart and the collective heart of others.

Finally, when relating personal experience, you must use the first person. Revert to "you," "they," or "one" and your message becomes an opinion rather than a reality, an example rather than an experience. Others might get the lesson, but they will miss the connection that is so vital to hearing your authentic voice.

Connecting with others—creating limbic resonance—is largely dependent on your choice to be vulnerable and authentic in what you communicate. The content of the message will determine what comes of that connection. The next chapters provide a framework for content, a guide for asking yourself the right questions to assure that your fundamental message platform is complete, and that it is both clear and deep.

6

Establish Competence and Build Trust

Three fundamental relationships underlie any leader-inspired change. We have been addressing one: that between you as the leader and the message. The relationship you are trying to affect is between other people and the message, so that people become committed to a cause voiced by you, the leader. Yet this commitment will happen only when the third and primary relationship, the one between you and those you hope to inspire, is based on competence and trust.

Trust is the fundamental requisite for people to listen to others without filters of fear or suspicion. Many who hold the position of leader, who sit in a corner office or have a title, make the mistake of thinking, "After all, I may be a bad communicator, but I am still the boss. They have to listen to me anyway." But people do not have to listen. Certain constituents may have to leave their backside in the seat while the boss talks, but real listening is not required. More important, people can never be required to act with any more conviction than it takes to go through the motions. *Required* action differs in both quantity and substance from *inspired* action.

Accordingly, communication about change starts with building credibility: a sense of your competence, and the feeling that you are trustworthy.

Establishing Competence

As you develop your message platform, there are questions that you have to ask yourself and answer to others. This platform stands on the elements that display competence: clear purpose and credentials.

Clarity of Purpose

What needs to change? What piece of compelling evidence do you have?

As a leader, you must have answers to these questions. To suggest the change, you have to consider it vital to progress. To support the change, you must have either objective evidence or observations that make it clear to you that there is a compelling need. To be authentic, you have to be able to state these elements strongly and explicitly at the beginning of the message and let others know that you are asking for change. Without being challenged to act, people will simply not engage. They may be entertained or bored, they might even be interested, but they will not engage. For this, you need a clear statement of purpose.

Franklin Raines, chairman and CEO of Fannie Mae, often carries the message that the African American effort for equality is not over. His purpose is, as he said in a speech to the Howard University graduating class, to identify racial gaps and determine why they exist and how we can close them. What is the compelling need? According to Raines, "If America had racial equality in education, and jobs, African Americans would have . . . two million more high school degrees, two million more college degrees, . . . and nearly $200 billion more income." The disparity that exists, shown by the numbers, totals "over $1 trillion in wealth."[1] Clear purpose, clear need.

Gaining clarity of purpose focuses your attention on your strongest conviction, and clarity of purpose focuses others' attention in a single direction. As it does, it begins to establish your own confidence, and their perception of competence in you, the leader.

Rebekah Saul Butler, a candidate for master's degrees in business and in public health at the University of California, developed this statement of purpose to anchor her leadership effort in encouraging more conscious end-of-life decisions: "End-of-life care is central to our national concern over the budget and the aging population, since almost 30 percent of all Medicare funds are spent in the last year of life. [Accordingly] I am going to advocate that we all have frank, open discussions in our families about these issues . . . about aging, death and dying, what they mean, and how you will confront them."[2]

Death is not an easy issue to deal with; clarity at the outset serves notice to everyone that we are entering difficult territory with some courage behind our conviction. The more difficult the issue, the more clarity is needed.

An advertising executive, Jim Losi, felt strongly about the power of diversity in his work group. As he prepared to lead this issue, he wrote out his intention to himself, articulating the importance as he saw it: "It's not my purpose to make anyone uncomfortable, but it *is* my purpose to engage this group with frank and sometimes personal communication. I want them to have a crystal clear understanding of the importance of this issue and be ready to take some personal action to deal with it. For most of the group, that will mean a change in the way they operate; but for many of them, it will also mean a change in the way they think."

Authentic decisiveness creates respect. Others' disagreement with a leader on an issue can be countered by that leader's willingness to engage truthfully and boldly. Accordingly, the more difficult the issue, the more desirable it is to be candid and forthright in formulating and stating your purpose. As a result of your strength, others will perceive a new possibility being created, and you will be marked as a person of principle, a person of strong conviction and of competence.

Political leaders know this principle well, and generally get their point of view out very early in any communication. Consider the first sentence of the text of Senator Edward Kennedy's prepared speech on Iraq in late 2002: "I have come here today to express my view that

America should not go to war against Iraq unless and until other reasonable alternatives are exhausted."[3]

Clear purpose and *strength* of purpose help establish competence, and compel others to engage.

Credentials for the Cause

What gives you the confidence that you are competent to lead this effort? Your competence to lead a given change with a given group is a function of your directly relevant work experience, life experience, and education, as well as additional credentials that might be important to the particular constituency. If you have the title of "leader" you might well have the authority to lead. But to follow your lead with commitment, people will need to know how you gained your competence in your chosen field.

Many of us are apt to underplay our credentials, either out of modesty or a belief that others should just know our background. But would you consider following anyone else's lead without knowing that individual's credentials? At the beginning of message development, you do have to consider your qualifications and be clear about them. You needn't highlight every bit of experience and education—just those that are especially meaningful to you and that would be meaningful to the group you are trying to lead. You then need to find a way to make the group aware of those qualifications to give them confidence in your ability.

Each culture recognizes certain general credentials that it considers fundamental to anyone's ability to lead. These may seem superficial, but in the early stages of a change effort, before others have had a chance to evaluate what you say or to hear your conviction on the subject, you need to establish a foothold of competence, just to open the group's collective mind to your leadership. In Europe, family history, social standing, and school ties are generally considered more important than in the United States, where life experience— what you've done on your own—might be considered more important than your alma mater. In the Far East, credentials are often established in some subtler way, to avoid the leader being perceived as self-serving.

Groups of people engaged in specific professions will also demand different evidence to demonstrate competence. An academic group will indeed be interested in your academic credentials, even if they are not directly related to the topic. But if you are leading a business group to take more risk, then work or life experience is far more valuable in establishing credibility. Bill Gates's or Steve Jobs's work experience is certainly adequate to establish their credibility, despite the fact that neither graduated from college.

A few years ago, Rob Nicholsen (the young environmentalist mentioned in Chapter Two) was developing a message to lead his peers in conservation. In preparing the base message, he included this statement of credentials:

> I have been extremely fortunate to have spent most of my life educating myself for my work. I have spent almost twenty-five years in schools and over thirty years in the outdoors. I've traveled from the Arctic Ocean to the Equator, climbed some of the highest peaks in Europe and trekked through the jungles of Borneo. As an environmental consultant for six years, I've visited more garbage dumps than I care to remember. I've been involved with oil spills off the coast of Alaska and train wrecks in densely populated urban areas.

His conclusion from all these experiences was that we are not living a sustainable existence and have to change the way we relate to our environment.

Rob's notations of credentials were not arrogant or self-serving. By formulating them, he was able to feel more powerful about the topic, as well as to prepare to simply and colorfully let others know what life experience, education, and work experience was relevant to his committed course of change. He intentionally referred to himself as "extremely fortunate," because he really felt that way. In the process of relating his experience, he did not set himself above others. This statement rather showed his real humility, and began to move him toward a deeper connection with his work and with others he hoped would participate.

Building Trust

With competence established through clarity and credentials, you can move toward establishing your trustworthiness. People trust others whom they know authentically, and who have their best interest at heart. The operative word is *authentically*. If you really don't care about others, if you have no urge or instinct to acknowledge them as you encourage change, you will not be able to gain their trust, even if you follow verbal conventions. Without caring, these conventions are simply rituals that sound good but allow people to avoid connection rather than facilitate it. These conventions were at one time meaningful, but like most formal expressions of a past experience, have since become only rules that we follow (usually unconsciously) to avoid real contact.

How many times have you heard or participated in this exchange?
"May I help you?"
"No thanks, I'm just looking."
Retail chains spend millions to get rid of this conventional conversation. In 2000, Safeway instituted a policy, openly mocked by many union members, that required check-out personnel to offer customers help to their cars and to call them by name. Rules such as these rarely help accomplish the objective. If the people staffing the check-out stands really want to serve, really want to connect, they will do so with no rules. Yet if retail salespeople aren't really interested in helping, it will come through without regard to what they say.

In many social situations, we use conventional words of acknowledgment to get us over the initial anxiety of meeting: a speaker saying "It's wonderful to be here tonight"; an auditor saying, "We're here to help" and the person being audited replying with "We're glad to see you." If you avoid using these conventions and instead enter into the relationship consciously, you can signal your intention to interact more authentically. I can illustrate.

In 1983, I was fortunate enough to meet with former president Jimmy Carter in Beverly Hills. My partner, Tom Green, and I were acting on behalf of some business and political leaders, promoting a very simple plan to relieve political tension between the United States and the Soviet Union. Carter had agreed to a short meeting to hear about it.

A Secret Service agent ushered us into the suite; Carter entered briskly shortly thereafter. Since Tom was standing closer to him, he shook Carter's hand first and said something like, "I am honored to meet you, Mr. President. You have been a real inspiration to me." Carter looked right at him and said, "Oh really, Tom, how's that?" I quickly ducked my head and waited for my partner to come up with something good, and in that painful ten seconds of silence that seemed like a day and a half, I learned a valuable lesson about appreciation. If it's real, it's written on your heart by experience, not on a piece of paper by convention. My partner's comment was real, he just had not reflected on *why* it was real.

Tom made a nice recovery, saying something about Carter's obvious deep partnership with Rosalyn and his courage in running for the presidency against heavy odds. When Carter shook my hand, I did not offer a gratuitous comment.

How many leaders could pass muster answering Carter's question? Imagine the host of a party stopping you after you have said "What a lovely home," with the comment: "Oh really, Tom, how's that?"

By learning how to acknowledge others authentically rather than conventionally, a leader can establish uncommon intimacy very quickly. Affirmation of others is the first principle of trust building, and includes the ability to authentically express gratitude and to acknowledge others' points of view. The second principle is being willing to be known and includes revealing your personal motivation and showing vulnerability.

Expressing Gratitude

Steve Farber, a fellow devotee of leadership and a superb public speaker, frequently asks his audience: "How many of you have ever received a note from someone expressing sincere appreciation?" Most in the audience will raise their hands. "How many of you still have that note?" Most will keep their hands up. He then asks how long the members of the audience have kept the notes. "Five years?" "Ten years?" Many hands remain up even as Steve asks, "Twenty-five years?" The record is *forty* years, and when Steve asked his respondent if he remembered what the note said, the person reached into his pocket and pulled the note from his wallet. After forty years, he still considered it one of his most prized possessions.

How many of us have kept a similar note? And for those of us who have, what is our opinion and feeling about the person who wrote it?

These are not rhetorical questions. The ability and willingness to express sincere appreciation is one of the most valuable skills of leadership communication. People will be inclined to follow others who make them feel good about themselves, who display an honest appreciation for who they are and what they do for the organization. As a leader, why not ask yourself what you are truly thankful for, with regard to this chance to communicate? Who—and what circumstance—can you authentically acknowledge as a gift?

It sounds simple, yet as the story of the notes indicates, the expression of sincere gratitude is rare and valuable. It is not easy to convey authentic appreciation; moreover, it is not considered important in a world where convention rather than authenticity rules most of our communication.

A few years ago, I was attending a program conducted by Brother David Steindl-Rast, a Benedictine monk and a prolific writer on gratefulness, a wonderful teacher, and a person I count as a rare, authentic human being. Brother David described an exercise that one of his teachers had prescribed for him as he was trying to understand gratitude. "For one year," said the teacher, "I want you to write two notes of gratitude before you leave your room in the morning."

"Easy enough," thought Brother David, until the teacher added, "and you have to experience the gratitude!"

We all know how to say "thank you," just as we know how to say "may I help you?" yet few of us consider how to generate the experience of being grateful. Unfortunately, unless we do generate that experience in ourselves, the object of our thanks will experience only the conventional and obligatory communication—"Thanks"—hardly a note worth keeping.

Leaders have to develop the capability of generating the experience of gratitude in themselves in order to engender the kind of loyalty displayed by those who keep notes for forty years.

I've tried the "don't leave your room until you feel grateful" exercise myself. It is enlightening, and enheartening. Should you try it, you would find that real gratitude is accessed from experience, not from rhetoric. From experience comes specificity and feelings, both generators of an authentic response. A friend and client, the late Ned Dean, was chairman of the Pacific Bank in 1994. He wanted to acknowledge one of his board members at a stockholders' meeting after a difficult two years. After several false starts and some coaching, he wrote the following, and later conveyed it to his stockholders:

> I want to give special thanks to Mark Hubbard, who attended more than fifty board and committee meetings last year, strictly out of his dedication to helping us turn the situation around. I remember one such occasion, about seven o'clock at night in the dead of winter, when I was leaving my office as Mark was coming in. He had just finished a day at his own company, and it was raining, a cold rain that would turn to snow in any other city. He had forgotten his umbrella, so his head was soaked as he came into the lobby. I actually felt guilty leaving so early. Now it's not as though Mark doesn't have other interests. He came to that meeting because he is dedicated, more as a friend of the company than as a board member. And he did it more than fifty times when we needed him most. I feel very lucky to have such friends serving all of us.

By reflecting on his specific experience, Ned was able to access real gratitude, not merely talk about conceptual gratitude. His authenticity moved the audience, Mr. Hubbard, and Ned himself, with more than information.

Karen Chang had a similar experience in conveying gratitude for her group of senior vice presidents of Schwab. These were people who had traveled extensively in the previous year, moving from branch to branch in a major change effort. Karen could have merely said, "I want to particularly express my appreciation to the senior vice presidents for their tireless efforts and extensive travel this last year." By convention, that would be acceptable. But rather than staying with convention, Karen did a bit of research and conveyed her feelings this way. "I want to particularly thank the senior vice presidents who made this happen by being on the road. They were gone from their homes an average of fifteen nights a month last year. All of them have families; and believe me, I know that a hundred and eighty nights is a lot of nights to go to bed without a hug from someone you love. I deeply appreciate them and their families for that."

Magic. She included herself, was specific, and made it real. Her feelings were obvious, as were the feelings of everyone else in the room. By conveying feelings that came from a real experience, she made the entire episode reflect what she wanted to reflect. Learning to express authentic gratitude is central to leadership communication; and the assignment can be enriching to everyone, including you, the leader.

Acknowledging Resistance

Your expressions of authentic gratitude will help others recognize your humanity but might do little to give them an experience of your empathy with their own points of view. Resistance and disagreement are natural responses to a call for change. Before making the call, you need to consider what people are thinking and feeling about this issue. You need to consider what their natural mental and emotional resistance to this change might be.

When Alfred Sloan, head of General Motors, was in a board meeting and an important decision was about to be made, he said, "I take it that everyone is in basic agreement with this decision." Everyone nodded in agreement. Sloan looked at the group and said,

"Then I suggest we postpone the decision. Until we have some disagreement, we don't understand the problem."[4]

As you build your message platform, considering other points of view or objections is important to your being able to think through the cogency of your own ideas. More important, it is central to being able to acknowledge others as a way of building trust.

Most of us fail to do this. We think through others' arguments, but we define them only as hurdles that we have to knock down to get our own way, rather than the reasonable points of view of others we hope to lead into a relationship of trust. Your strong statements of purpose will of course amplify feelings and ideas of resistance in others, and will probably provoke expressions of discontent. But these contrary ideas and feelings of discontent are present whether you acknowledge them or not. By bringing them to the surface, you establish your ability to be empathetic, and you demonstrate your willingness to become a partner rather than an adversary. By shining light on these thoughts and feelings early, you maintain and reinforce your motivation. In fact, recognizing resistance as normal gives you yet another chance to create real limbic resonance with others, to connect with their hearts and not just their minds.

Conversely, if you pretend that acceptance of your new proposal will come without uncertainty, you will lose your credibility and risk being undermined, and you will never gain the full commitment of others. They may *comply*, but their resistance will manifest itself in negativity and an absence of energy for the task at hand. Resistance not dealt with will continue to thrive, not only as others listen to your comments but also in the halls, bathrooms, highways, and homes where people say what has not been said in your presence.

Unfortunately, those with the most resistance to your ideas will frequently avoid expressing it. Few people are willing to risk the disapproval of a leader by actually voicing doubts about a new direction, and the stronger their objections, the more intense their fear. Instead, those reservations are only expressed to those the leader loves, respects, and trusts. Accordingly, it is your responsibility to create an atmosphere that will honor dissenting views and feelings. Only by doing so can you maintain the respect and positive engagement of those you lead. By acknowledging resistance, you are acknowledging *reality* and maintaining the aura of authenticity.

I first heard of this idea from Harvey Stone, an excellent speech coach and writer in Santa Fe, New Mexico. Harvey used the example of a domestic "discussion," in which a couple is in heated exchange, sometimes for days, until one of them (Harvey says that in his house, it is most often his wife) acknowledges the other's feelings and opinions. Imagine yourself in a combative mood, as your adversary stops, pauses, and says: "You know, I didn't realize that you felt so strongly about this issue. You sound as though you feel hurt, and I know that you honestly disagree with my point of view."

There is no *agreement* in this statement, only honest *noticing* and *honoring* of some strong feelings and a different opinion. While the discussion certainly isn't over, one can feel the adverse energy drain out of the situation, such that ears might be open to hear for the first time in the "discussion." This same release occurs whenever negative feelings and opinions are acknowledged. The respect voiced by the leader for other points of view can open the minds of dissenters as the leader's motivation becomes less suspect. Such acknowledgment does not guarantee agreement with your position, but it will dissipate the argumentative energy and open the possibility of honest dialogue.

Rational Resistance and Cynicism

The easiest resistance to suspend is based on misunderstanding. The leader simply has information that others do not have. Others may be cynical about the proposed change because it (or perhaps something that sounds like it) has been tried before, or they may be fearful of change because of their lack of knowledge. Such resistance can be considered and acknowledged in the beginning of any message. It can be refuted later, but in the spirit of common understanding rather than argument.

What does this look like?

In developing his message platform for a change in supply chain management, John Ure of Agilent was suggesting a new focus on customers, a holistic approach that would create an integration of the supply chain. He made the following notes about resistance:

> When thinking about this new way, I can hear voices, my own included, that argue, from Marketing, "I already focus on the customer, although perhaps not to the point of actual intimacy, so why the need to change?" or from Purchasing, "I have already developed excellent partnership with our suppliers, why do we need to change?" or from Design, "Don't come and tell me how to design a product, I am perfectly competent, just get on with getting the best price." Indeed we do all of those things, and I don't want to lose this focus, this partnership, or this competency in design.

These notes on resistance do not, in themselves, *refute* the resistance. They merely help John and others know that he was under no illusions about their points of view. In fact, he acknowledged his own resistance at the same time ("my own included"). When the other players realized that John knew about their doubts and was open to them, they were, in kind, open to hear what else he had to say, and they were willing to engage with him, knowing that he could acknowledge their point of view.

The same thinking can be applied to selling, to promoting a new product to a large audience of potential consumers.

David Craford, a sales executive with Affymetrix in California's Silicon Valley, was a leader in advocating acceptance and use of bioengineered food. He realized that many people were legitimately fearful of such food, and acknowledged that resistance in his message development: "I know that a few people have doubts about this technology, they might well be afraid of putting 'bioengineered' foods into their body or having them grown in their fields. I understand these concerns. It's important for us to have a common understanding of how this technology works, and why we need it to work on a local and global level."

Again, David could not possibly eliminate all the fears surrounding bioengineered foods. What he could do, however, was to anticipate others' thoughts and feelings as preparation for letting them know early that he appreciated their point of view. This opened an opportunity for them to hear what he had to say with their strong feelings suspended, and to engage with him as a leader, not merely as a contrarian.

Resistance based on a different or inadequate understanding of the facts can be relieved with explanation. John Ure went on to address the resistance later in his message, by explaining the difference in his new plan and the status quo, and David Craford explained the methods of development for high-tech tomatoes, using common metaphors to educate others and assuage their fears.

Irrational Resistance

Other resistance comes not from any lack of understanding but from incorrect and entrenched beliefs. Such resistance cannot be corrected logically. It's important that you, as leader, realize this and not yield to indignation. Although most people who hold onto such beliefs are not good candidates for partnership and may well leave the organization, if you understand and acknowledge their point of view, you may create an atmosphere in which some of them listen rather than withdraw.

Consider the following comments from Jim Losi's message platform on diversity, referred to earlier in this chapter. His company was launching an initiative on the need for more diversity in the workforce. This is a particularly emotional issue in Jim's industry, which has traditionally been dominated by white males. After introducing the subject, Jim made the following notes on resistance:

> Some people may still wonder why this topic is getting so much attention; they may still think that it is a response to government regulation or that it is *only* a moral issue that supports our values as a company. Frankly, a year ago, I might have held similar misconceptions. But after a year on the task force, reading demographic predictions, and thinking about the future of our company, I have a considerably different view.
>
> Some of them also might be threatened by the issue. Those in the majority might feel that it means less opportunity, or an

institution of quotas. Some of them might still be under the illusion that increasing diversity will lower standards.

Those who see themselves as *not* a member of the majority might feel that the issue puts unreasonable attention on them, that they might be viewed as needing special attention, or that it is their task to educate the majority.

These are understandable fears, but they are *only* fears. *Some* of them might be justified by reality. *None* of them is a reason not to move forward.

Jim was able, in this statement, to acknowledge the fears, respect others' points of view, and challenge them to move forward anyway. Like all leadership issues, Jim's topic dealt with a suggested course of action to change the status quo. He is calling on others in the company for trust, asking them to progress *through* their fears to a new future. Understanding and acknowledging their resistance is another step in establishing authentic conviction about change.

Gratitude and the acknowledgment of resistance lead others to gauge if the leader truly has their interest at heart. The motivation of the leader is still a critical element in developing trust.

Personal Motivation

To agree to action, people want to know why a change is important to the organization and how they will benefit from it. But to commit to follow a leader down an uncertain path, they have to know the leader's personal motivation. Personal motivation is central to trustworthiness. It doesn't have to do with material outcome, it has to do with meaning. "I have a dream," was Martin Luther King Jr.'s personal motivation. Examining your own and revealing it is part of building trust.

The best example I've ever heard of this aspect of earning trust was brought to my attention by Peter Alduino, a leadership consultant from Santa Cruz. He found a videotape, made in 1974, of the late Barbara Jordan. Jordan was then an African American member of the U.S. House of Representatives, from Texas, and on the tape was speaking to the committee hearing the evidence to impeach former President Nixon. As a junior member of the committee, she spoke for fifteen minutes, including this prologue:

> Earlier today, we heard the beginning to the preamble to the Constitution of the United States . . . "we the people," a very eloquent beginning. But when that document was completed on the 17th of September in 1787, I was not included in "we the people."
>
> I felt somehow for many years that George Washington and Alexander Hamilton just left me out by mistake. But through the process of amendment, interpretation and court decision, I have finally been included in "we the people."
>
> Today I am an inquisitor, and hyperbole would not be fictional and would not overstate the solemnness that I feel right now. My faith in the Constitution is whole, it is complete, it is total. And I am not going to sit here and be an idle spectator to the diminution, the subversion, the destruction of the Constitution.[5]

There is no question about Jordan's personal motivation, and any constituent who felt equally disenfranchised would be inspired by her statement. Notice that it is personal, not theoretical, not talking about people in general. Jordan did not say, "We should be diligent in protecting the Constitution, because it is the basis of our freedom as a nation." Although she certainly would agree with that statement, her personal motivation is what creates the platform for her very personal leadership on this issue.

Meaning is conveyed when we can connect our actions to our personal values. Sometimes that is done with a story, as when I realized the connection between delivering kids to college and delegation. While on a different scale, the experience made delegation meaningful for me, just as Barbara Jordan's very intense personal experience made the health of the Constitution meaningful for her.

Many might think that this connection can't be made in a business environment, but consider the story of Howard Schultz that I related in Chapter Two. Schultz was very clear about his personal motivation for building Starbucks into the kind of company it is, where everyone feels like a partner. His experience with his father drove his values to the surface, and he was able to express them later in his business. Schultz's revelation carried with it not only his personal motivation but the aura of vulnerability that brings others close.

Relevant Vulnerability

The final element of building trust is knowing and acknowledging what you *don't* bring to the table. An honest assessment of your capabilities and limitations reinforces the insight that others are interacting with a real human being, and brings an uncommon sense of trust to relationships. As you begin developing your message of change, reflect on your shortcomings. What are you trying to become better at? What will people assume about you that simply isn't true? Write it down, and reflect on how you can reveal it.

Mario Cuomo was a champion of abortion rights as a matter of public policy. But he was also a practicing Catholic. He was asked to address the combined faculty and administration of Notre Dame on the subject, and found it the perfect opportunity to think through and ferret out his own thinking and feeling on this subject in a way that he had not before. The address that he eventually gave formed the basis for his extemporaneous remarks on the subject of the relationship of his faith to his public policy for the rest of his career. Considering the audience for this speech, and his constituents in general, he felt the need to tell them directly who he was and who he was not. As he said:

> Let me begin this part of the effort by underscoring the obvious. I do not speak as a theologian, I do not have that competence. I do not speak as a philosopher; to suggest that I could would be to set a new record for false pride. I don't presume to speak as a "good" person except in the ontological sense of that word . . . [rather], I speak here as a politician. And also as a

Catholic, a layperson baptized and raised in the pre-Vatican II church, educated in Catholic schools, attached to the church first by birth, then by choice, now by love. An old-fashioned Catholic who sins, regrets, struggles, worries, gets confused, and most of the time feels better after confession. The Catholic church is my spiritual home. My heart is there, and my hope.[6]

Aside from the beautiful words, the content of this supplementary self-introduction did far more for Cuomo's credibility with this audience than the fact that he was a governor who wrestled with public policy every day. He established his connection with this audience as a human being by including his personal motivation to speak and his personal vulnerabilities. Despite the fact that he was advocating a position very unpopular with this group, he was going to be trusted.

You cannot be the expert on all the mechanisms necessary to effect major change. You can, however, acknowledge those shortcomings without giving up your ability to lead. In fact, you will enhance your own credibility, giving others clear signals about their potential contribution.

Here is John Ure's commentary about his own supply chain expertise: "If any think I'm new to this field, they'd be right. I don't profess to be a purchasing expert. . . . I have zero time served in this discipline. I don't profess to be a supply chain guru, or a quality systems expert. Indeed my eyes start glazing over when I hear some of you talking about the areas in which you do have these skills."

As you may have surmised, vulnerability is the flip side of credentials. Clear purpose, credentials, vulnerability, personal motivation, expressing gratitude, and acknowledging others' points of view—these are all aspects of a leadership communication that you need to ponder and record before you move into the issue itself. And of course, these are all aspects of emotional intelligence, and your willingness to consider them supports your decision to lead, not just dictate, change. Your relationship to those you hope to inspire and your relationship to the message you hope to deliver have to be clear and deep for you to be perceived as an authentic leader, both competent and personally trustworthy. Once you have completed this thinking, you have a chance of gaining real, committed support. The beginning of this message platform sets the tone and the limits for the leader and those the leader wishes to engage, inviting them to entertain change. The degree of both confidence and trust that develops between you and others will be determined by the authenticity you can transmit. The tone of your credentials, the way in which you show appreciation for your listeners, the strength of your purpose, the empathy you portray for their resistance and the cost and benefit they perceive in your advocacy—each of these elements will affect their willingness to engage.

After you have included these rudiments, you need to record your perspective, the story that compels you to seek change at all, this change in particular, and to do it now.

Questions to Ask in Building Trust and Establishing Competence

Clarity of Purpose

- What problem needs to be solved—specifically?
- What needs to change?
- What pieces of compelling evidence do I have? What is the overriding piece of compelling evidence that something needs to change?

Credentials

- What gives me confidence that I am competent to lead this effort?
- What life experience, work experience, or portion of my education is relevant?
- What will my constituents need to know about me to be confident in my leadership?   (*continued*)

Gratitude

- What am I truly thankful for, with regard to this chance to communicate or those with whom I will interact?

- What circumstance, group, or individual can I authentically acknowledge as a gift?

Acknowledging Resistance

- How can I demonstrate my interest in others?

- What are people thinking and feeling about this issue?

- What will be their natural mental and emotional resistance to this change?

- What objective resistance do others have?

- What emotions will likely be present in others?

- What commonality do we share?

- What aspirations do we share?

Personal Motivation

- Why does this issue matter to me personally?

- What story could demonstrate my conviction?

- What personal value is represented by this change?

- Am I taking a stand about a principle that is important to me?

- What core principles, values, or beliefs motivate me to want to resolve this fairly, with everyone's interest being served?

Relevant Vulnerability

- What is it that I don't know?

- What are the areas in which I don't yet have expertise with regard to this issue?

- What help will I need?
- What mistakes might I have made with regard to this issue or with this group that I could acknowledge?
- What obstacles are in this for me personally?
- What are some personal qualities that I could convey to others that would allow them to connect with me as a human being?

7

Create Shared Context

Change occurs when it is time. A leader notices that history has pointed the way toward change and by communicating makes the direction of change obvious to others. Where we've been points to where we are, which points to where we are going. When people see this story as the leader sees it, they will have an understanding that the time is right for change. They might even decide that change is needed on their part. They will not yet, however, be committed to contributing to make it happen.

As you tell the story of where you and your constituents have been and where you are now, you are accomplishing three purposes. First, you are establishing a common understanding of events leading up to the status quo. This common understanding becomes the foundation for a *decision* to change. Second, you are presenting a view of the issue that is broader than the self-interest of the audience and large enough to hold the change you are advocating. You are offering the audience a chance to be a part of something *unchangeable*, something larger than themselves. Third, you are continuing to reinforce others' sense of your *competence* and their feelings of *trust* in you.

When you and your constituents have a common understanding of the context, change is a natural outcome. But most often, others haven't thought about the context that you have considered, that you know to be true; they need to be informed of it to make sense of what you are saying.

Building a Common Understanding of History

The need for shared context seems obvious. A story from one of my favorite spiritual writers, the late Henri Nouwen, demonstrates the importance of context to those who are listening but who have no experience themselves. Nouwen was a Catholic priest, mystic, and teacher. One of his works, *The Genesee Diary*, recounts his experience during a seven-month sabbatical inside the cloisters of the Trappist monastery at Genesee. For the monks, there were no newspapers, television, or other means of finding out what was going on in the world. Only the proctor (in this case, Father Marcellus) was privy to the *New York Times*.

Vespers in the monastery include the mentioning of "prayer intentions" by the monks. Nouwen reported the following occurrence:

> On one particular evening, Father Marcellus said, "Let us pray for the wife of the President of South Korea" . . . then he realized that nobody except he had read the latest newspaper, and quickly added . . . "who was assassinated" . . . then it probably flashed through his mind that nobody could understand why anyone would want to assassinate the wife of the President of South Korea, so he added . . . "while someone was trying to assassinate the President himself" . . . then he realized that by now the monks wanted to know the end of the story, so he concluded his intention with the words . . . "who safely escaped!"[1]

Although most of us are not speaking to people as cloistered as monks in a monastery, others are indeed cloistered in their own reality; the need for creating a new context remains. In the worlds of business and geopolitics, continuous instability and a plethora of media messages prevent many from knowing the real context and thereby determining the value of change. Very few people are willing to commit to change without first receiving a substantial education. As a leader, you have to inform people of the context, and then remind them, again and again. If you do not do so, your suggested change will be seen as meaningless or nonsensical. Context answers the question, Why?

I was on a trip to the Far East when an aspiring Japanese MBA candidate engaged me in conversation in Japan's First Bank of Commerce. We had just heard a lecture about the changing relationship between Japanese banks and their customers. The young man explained to me that for the last fifty years, Japanese banks and their commercial business customers were partners with the Japanese government. The incentives for industry and financial service entities had clearly remained the same over that period. Regulations, however, were now changing to give banks and their commercial customers some different motivations. Accordingly, customers were no longer willing to accept the judgment of the bank without question. For the first time, the bank was being asked by customers to justify currency trades made on their behalf that turned out badly. In the absence of common goals, customers needed to know why banks make these currency trades. To respond, the bank started a series of training classes for their customers to explain the vagaries of currency trading. They took the responsibility of articulating the context for their customers.

Later in the same conversation, the young man told me that the identical problem exists between the older generation in the bank and his own peers. "The veterans have the benefit of the old culture, and we do not. Consequently, we do not understand the reason for their actions." This contextual misunderstanding was far greater than the reasons for making certain trades. In this case, the leaders of the bank had not shared the context of the historical linkages between banks, their long-time customers, and the government. Such connections run very deep and are based on the fundamental pillars of the interconnected Japanese culture and economy. Because this young man and others like him had gone to school in the West, they were unfamiliar with these roots. The reason that was absent for the young was based on unspoken understandings of the past and their results in the present, a connection that was not communicated by his elders.

By explaining the why of currency trading to its customers, this bank assured their continued loyalty. But without the why of the Japanese business culture, the young Japanese employee will perform his duties without meaning, never developing any loyalty to the institution.

This same generational issue exists in nearly every culture, as baby boomers reach their peak leadership years and try to communicate with employees or constituents who grew up not knowing the Beatles, never being without a computer or e-mail, and—for some—having global travel experiences before they were of legal age. Others have not had the benefits of computers or travels, and come from a context of tattoos, shrinking possibilities, and no vision of a future beyond their current circumstances.

In preparing a change message platform, you have to consider the background, examine the history of the issue, think through the broad implications of change, and reflect on the moral consequences. Your constituents have not looked at the issue so thoroughly; they have not traced the issue to its conclusion, nor have they examined the history leading up to change. Like the young Japanese student, they do not have the benefit of seeing this issue against the background of the old culture.

The same opportunity exists, of course, for young leaders. The boomer generation you might be depending on for financing, consulting, or operations expertise might not have the benefit of your fresh approach or your more global understanding. One of your jobs as leader is to provide that information by communicating your perspective.

Developing a Broader, More Meaningful View

Many times, people have not seen the historical facts, the story, in a view broad enough to allow them to take part in something new, far-reaching, and meaningful—something larger than themselves. When a leader sees a circumstance in a larger, more meaningful context and is willing to explain it, that leader is in fact *creating* the context, calling everyone's attention to the idea that the context is greater than what first appears. Certainly this was the case when Thomas Jefferson declared, "We hold these truths to be self-evident, that all men are created equal, that they are endowed by their Creator with certain unalienable Rights, that among these are Life, Liberty and the pursuit of Happiness."

Before this declaration, there were no such things as "human rights." Kings had rights, people with land had rights, but there were no rights that accrued to people merely on the basis of their humanness. Jefferson created the context of human rights that has been one of the bases of U.S. foreign policy ever since. It is no small wonder that other nations might see the United States as naïve or idealistic if they have no such context in their own country. We can certainly do better in explaining this context internationally. Context becomes the reason to suspend the rules of the old game in favor of a larger one.

The world of baseball gave us a solid lesson in the significance of context during one of the pastime's most famous games. Fans get chills at the mention of a "perfect game"—a game in which the pitcher has been successful in getting every batter on the opposing team out three times in nine innings. Not one player from the other team reaches first base. A perfect game is a *very* rare occurrence.

Only one such game has ever been pitched in the World Series of baseball. The late Stephen Jay Gould, natural scientist and author, related the story in *The Flamingo's Smile*. He credited a *New York Times* op-ed piece of November 10, 1984:

> What could be more elusive than perfection? And what would you rather be . . . the agent or the judge? Babe Pinelli (who died at age 89 at a convalescent home near San Francisco) was the umpire in baseball's unique episode of perfection when it mattered most. October 8, 1956. A perfect game in the World Series . . . and coincidentally, Pinelli's last official game as arbiter. What a consummate swan song. Twenty-seven men to the plate, and twenty-seven men down. And,

since single acts of greatness are intrinsic spurs to democracy, the agent was a competent, but otherwise undistinguished Yankee pitcher, Don Larsen.

The dramatic end was all Pinelli's, and controversial ever since. Dale Mitchell, pinch hitting for Sal Maglie, was the twenty-seventh batter. With a count of 1 ball and 2 strikes, Larsen delivered one high and outside . . . close, but surely not, by its technical definition, a strike. Mitchell let the pitch go by, but Pinelli didn't hesitate. Up went the right arm for called strike three. Out went Yogi Berra from behind the plate, nearly tackling Larsen in a frontal jump of joy. "Outside by a foot," groused Mitchell later. He exaggerated . . . for it was outside by only a few inches . . . but he was right.

Babe Pinelli, however, was more right. A batter may not take a close pitch with so much on the line. *Context matters*. Truth is a circumstance, not a spot.

Truth is inflexible. Truth is inviolable. By long and recognized custom, by any concept of justice, Dale Mitchell had to swing at anything close. It was a strike . . . a strike high and outside. Babe Pinelli, umpiring his last game, ended with his finest, his most perceptive, his most truthful moment. Babe Pinelli, arbiter of history, walked into the locker room and cried.[2]

Babe Pinelli was able to break the rules of a national pastime by virtue of the universally understood context of the game of baseball and the circumstances of this particular game. Had the game been played at mid-season, with little at stake, he would have called the pitch a ball. Or, had he called a strike, there would have been cries of disagreement. In this case, in this context, the leader stated the truth, and the change was agreed to instantly by everyone in the park, everyone who was glued to a radio, and I would bet, even by Dale Mitchell.

This application of this principle to baseball is American, but the application to business and politics is global. The idea of shared context is easy to see among baseball fans, even easier among citizens of the United States; and as we are seeing, it is more challenging when we apply the principle to the citizens of the world. There are few universally common contexts, and that fact is a major challenge for global leaders. Most just do not perceive a large enough scale.

Peter Senge, in researching *The Fifth Discipline*, found that a profound sense of scale was common to inspirational leaders. "Each [leader]," says Senge, "perceived a deep story and sense of purpose that lay behind his vision, what we have come to call the *purpose story*—a larger 'pattern of becoming' that gives unique meaning to his personal aspirations and his hopes for their organization."[3] This language might seem ethereal, but Senge suggests that reflection on your own personal values will yield a broader and more personal context for your role as leader. Communicating this larger "purpose story" invites others to become a part of something larger than themselves, giving them a chance to make a difference in a bigger arena than they have perceived possible. The leader is giving others the opportunity to trade their commitment for greatness. Nearly all consider this a very good bargain.

Consider the fact that Nobel Laureate Stephen Hawking's first book, *A Brief History of Time*, has sold nearly 6 million copies in thirty languages since its publication in 1989. This is somewhat astounding, when you consider that according to the author, to read and understand this book (an explanation of the search for a unifying theory for the origin and working of the universe) would qualify the reader to start a Ph.D. in theoretical physics. Many explanations have been offered for the book's unanticipated popularity. Hawking, however, thinks the reason is simply that the general public wants to be involved in the discussion of "really big questions."

I agree. Many leaders—in all fields, particularly politics—are too quick to patronize their public, assuming that they are either selfish, dull, or uninterested in global or universal questions. Quite the contrary, the public is eager to hear, eager to engage, and eager to act when called to contribute to causes that are larger than themselves, even when they don't understand the details. All monumental changes that eventually occur originally seem to be *too* great, *too* challenging, *too* costly. In recent times, the destruction of the Berlin

Wall, the reunification of Germany, the end of apartheid in South Africa, the beginning of nuclear disarmament, all these great changes seemed beyond reach. Yet each one was accomplished by ordinary people sharing the vision, and seeing the context, of a leader. The confidence of today's public can only be strengthened by leaders who can present change as a chance for others to have an impact on a scale that is much larger than the immediate and obvious. As the interconnectedness of the world grows clearer, the scale of impact simply must become larger. This is a major challenge of our time. Few leaders have the perspective to make this shift.

Reinforcing Competence and Trust

This context section of the message also affords opportunities to strengthen competence and trust that you have established earlier. Competence is reinforced with evidence, which I discuss briefly here and more broadly in Appendix A. But trust can also be reinforced. Your vision *is* personal, your motivations *are* for the common good, and these as well as your competence can be reinforced by including your experience within the context of the message.

Thomas Jefferson lived in the context of "when in the course of human events." He felt the oppression of the British, personally ex-perienced the frustration of taxes that he paid without representa-tion. So it was with Gandhi, Barbara Jordan, Martin Luther King Jr., Nelson Mandela, and Joan of Arc. Because they lived in their own context, they rarely had to speak of it, but it was clear that they were affected by the history of the issue, and knowledge of that fact made their motivations clearer, their competence more obvious.

So it is with you. Even if the change you are advocating might seem less significant than the changes led by these icons, the princi-ples of inspiration are the same. Letting others know your personal historical experience with the change that you are advocating might not strengthen the logical case for the mind, but it will compel the heart to listen as well. The mind makes a decision based on agreement with the information the speaker provides. The heart makes the commitment based on a feeling of connection to the leader. The mind looks for evidence, the heart looks for passion. The mind weighs facts, the heart acts on faith. The mind looks for purpose, the heart seeks meaning. The mind believes, the heart trusts. Both are necessary for committed action.

Creating a common understanding, providing a broader view of the opportunity, and reinforcing trust and competence—these are the purposes of communicating context. Let's look at some examples.

John Adams, then chairman and CEO of Texas Commerce Bank, was a powerful advocate for corporate adoption of practices that supported families, particularly working mothers. He delivered a speech to the National Council of Jewish Women in 1993 and later published it as a way of spreading his message. After stating the purpose, Adams continued by asking the contextual question explicitly:

Why are corporate leaders more and more addressing work-family issues in their business planning and management?

One obvious reason is the changing family. When the drive to American industrial dominance began to build steam in the '50s, the country was comfortable with the notion of a working husband and a wife at home with kids. It made sense in the wake of World War II. The men had come home. Rosie the Riveter could leave the factory. They both wanted children, and American prosperity enabled single-earner families to lead comfortable lives.

Today, we must deal with new realities. Remember the guy who wouldn't dream of his wife working. He's the same guy who now wakes her up in the middle of the night to suggest that she ask her boss for a raise.

Fewer than 22 percent of married-couple households consist of a male breadwinner and female homemaker. In the 1950s, the figure was 80 percent.

Fifty-eight percent of mothers with children under six now hold paying jobs. The figure was 20 percent in 1960.

And 68 percent of mothers with children under 18 work out-side the home.

Today, the majority of families rely on two incomes to maintain a middle-class standard of living, and a significant number of families need two incomes just to pull themselves above the poverty line. Two working parents, and single par-ents, bring an array of needs with them into the workforce that didn't exist before.[4]

How does this context stack up against our criteria? Certainly, the historical context is well done. There is no question that this particular group (The National Council of Jewish Women) would have a firm grasp on the history of the issue. Adams has told them where they have been and where they are, and has let them know why it's necessary to break the established rules of work.

He has also broadened the issue to one of values that are greater than an individual agenda. This change is clearly the "right thing to do" in light of the rights of women, and the newer definition of the family, and the relationship of corporations to their employees.

Has he reinforced his own personal competence and trustwor-thiness? Has he established himself as a leader rather than a mere carrier of information?

Not really.

We don't know anything about his own personal involvement in this context. As a middle-aged man he might well have had parents who lived in the old world. His mother might well have been a "Rosie the Riveter" who came home from the factory. His own children might well be in the current generation, coupled with mates who work in commerce and try to balance their families with their other obligations. We simply don't know. As he developed this message, which resulted in this same speech being given in several venues, he could have considered adding such details, which would convert a mere set of facts to a personal reflection on those facts and thereby raised his stature to a leader, rather than a mere presenter of data.

Anita Roddick, former managing director of The Body Shop, omitted the other aspect of evidence as she established the following context in a speech to the International Chamber of Commerce. Roddick has been an outspoken leader of the effort to establish permanent beachheads of capital investment in underdeveloped countries.

> There is always someplace in the world that is a little worse off, where the living conditions are a little wretched. Just look at industry after industry in search of even lower wages and looser standards. From Europe or the U.S. to Taiwan to Malaysia. Each country is just another pit stop in the race to the bottom. The new frontier is China, where wages and environmental standards are still lower and human rights abuses even more sordidly suppressed. The new nomadic capital never sets down roots, never builds communities; it leaves behind toxic wastes and embittered workers.
>
> You may think this is hyperbole. Please go out and check. Visit the cities capital flight has left behind in the U.S. and England. Go to the places I have been around the world where capital has newly—and temporarily—alighted. Hold the mutated babies, genetically handicapped by toxic wastes dumped in local streams. Meet the indigenous communities being driven out of existence.[5]

Anita Roddick has produced a marvelous personal context in this speech. We see her personal statement of *the history* of the global cost of a capitalist free-for-all, and *her* own personal experience of the broad negative impact of trade unrestricted by care for human values. Just as with John Adams's audience, those who hear her are called to change things that are larger than their own short-term interest. When she developed the message that resulted in this speech, she was aware of her own feelings and experience, but she shorted us on the facts. We don't really know the history of the issue that gives rise to the change, but we might feel as though she is the right person to be leading us down this path.

An appeal to values taps the humanity of others. If the change you want will legitimately make life better for others, if it will help people make a difference in the world, then they will respond, whether you are asking for better customer service or assistance to the poor. If you have experience in the realm of such "difference making," relating it will enhance your trustworthiness. But experience alone is also not enough. Data, such as Adams's evidence, enhances your reputation for competence, but only if others hear it and find it accurate and relevant.

Choosing Evidence: Showing the Logic

Evidence to support a given point of view is abundant, and you, as the leader, no longer have privileged access to that evidence. Clearly, the amount of information to be known is accelerating at a rate substantially faster than anyone's ability to know it, and accessing that information is becoming easier. The world's public, even in the most remote regions, has a wealth of data available.

I was trekking and traveling in the country of Bhutan for more than a month in 2001. This idyllic nation, protected by the Himalayas and its strategic position, remains a bastion of Tibetan Buddhism. The political power is shared by a king and the head of the body of monks. Citizens wear the national dress, and the countryside is streaked with flowing rivers even Montanans would envy. Perennial forests range to fourteen thousand feet, and rhododendrons grow taller than a two-story house, decorating the green conifers. Each village is self contained; life seems as though it takes place in Shangri-La. Bhutan's representative gave a speech to the United Nations in 1998 declaring that the country was actually measuring "Gross National Happiness," rather than GNP.

Yet even in what is perhaps the last stronghold of a nature-based culture, the Internet and CNN invade. Despite a plurality of opinion that the culture should eschew information technology, Bhutan is about to become "twice born." In every guest house and hotel, Indian video is the entertainment of choice. Internet cafés dot Thimpu, its capital, and even its minor villages. The march of information, available to nearly everyone, moves on. Not all of this information is accurate, of course, but its availability gives everyone a new reference point to measure the competence of anyone who advocates change.

As you build your message, you will obviously do the research. For a leader looking to inspire, the evidence you use and the way in which you use it are both vital to maintaining credibility.

In Appendix A, you will find a complete discussion of the rules of evidence in leadership communication: that specifics encourage engagement, that relevance to others is critical to evidence being given "weight," and that quotations from experts can be distracting or attracting, depending on how well such experts are known to you and to others.

Ultimately, data, examples, and the voices of other authorities serve as excellent evidence for the mind. They help fulfill the first requirement for context: to create a common understanding of the circumstances that led up to the current situation. Expansion of the meaning of change and the bond of competence and trustworthiness are both generated by your own personal involvement with the context and by your own experience with the evidence that you present.

Revealing the Personal: Showing the Passion

Once you and others have agreed on a context, you have also agreed on the need for change. You have mutually defined the chasm to be jumped. But to be willing to jump this chasm with you, others must be convinced of your competence and satisfied that you are trustworthy. In contrast to your competence, your trustworthiness is subjective. It will be answered in the personal experiences, analogies, metaphors, and stories that you use to support your own authenticity.

I recently visited Singapore to do some work with a client. On a day off, I found myself near the waterfront in a downtown bank plaza. Standing before me was a fifteen-foot-tall Salvador Dali bronze, "Homage to Newton," an abstract figure of a human featuring large holes in the skull and chest. A bronze heart is suspended from fine wire in the center of the body and a brain is carved to appear suspended in the skull. The explanatory plaque indicates that it is by expressing both mind and heart that all of human enterprise is accomplished. This is, indeed, the challenge of today's leaders. Inspiring committed action requires the speaker to appeal to *both* the heart and the mind.

We don't often do it well. To many potential leaders, particularly those trained as lawyers or business professionals, the context of a change message is where one proves the case. Particularly in Western culture, the "proof" is considered sacrosanct, and when others ignore this proof they are considered either incapable of grasping the truth or irresponsible. Yet each day, we see juries making decisions that seem to be totally unjustified by the facts of the case. The jurors have looked for holes in the judge's instructions that will allow them to return a verdict consistent with the direction their collective hearts lead them. To ignore this phenomenon, to disregard our ability and desire to enlarge our experience of life to include the facts and move beyond them, is to fail to lead. The jury is merely the most obvious case of proof not necessarily dictating action. Certainly there are others. For example, public policy decisions that seem logical don't get implemented because compassionate people on the front lines see their impact on those they serve. In other instances, decisions by corporate executives, steeped in logic, don't get carried out at the operational level.

Is it cynicism? Apathy? Inertia? Or are people just taking action despite the logic of the situation? Whatever the motivation, people are acknowledging new ways of deciding and taking appropriate action. We are not willing to merely connect all the logical, digital dots to form the picture; we want to draw outside the lines of the strategic mind and acknowledge the analog, flowing nature of life to help us live appropriately. This may not be in the corporate rule book—but it is very human.

Blaise Pascal, seventeenth-century mathematician, had a running argument with René Descartes about the axiom Descartes favored, "I think, therefore I am." The conflict was often bitter, but when Pascal became ill, Descartes attended him as a physician and stayed with him for long periods of time. When Pascal asked about his reasoning for staying with and caring for such a long-time rival, Descartes replied, "The heart has reasons that reason knows nothing of."[6]

Completing the Context

Earlier, we reviewed the purpose statement in messages developed by Rebekah Saul Butler, of Berkeley. Her interest is in encouraging families to have discussions about death and dying before the event, to make sure that the emotional and economic realities are clear. Rebekah was concerned—on both the personal and the national level—about a meaningful process of death, and about the implications of long-term care on national policy and economics. This is a tough issue to lead; so to begin, she documented her own personal context, revealing the source of her passion:

> When I was a young girl, my grandfather grew ill with heart disease. Lucky for us, he was saved by bypass surgery. He then survived eleven great years, living very well, enjoying his grandchildren and his retirement. Over time he grew sick again with heart disease and with Parkinson's. His quality of life was poor and he was in pain. He almost died one weekend and the family flew in, pressed his suit, and wrote his obituary, when my grandfather's doctor decided to try one more heart medication and my grandfather responded. He lived two more years in a nursing home, sometimes strapped to his bed because he wanted to go home so badly he would try to crawl out of the window at night, and because the medication for his Parkinson's disease made him hallucinate and he was often frightened. When I visited him in the nursing home, I often wondered if we had made the right decisions for him. Prior to his health crisis, we had not talked in depth about end-of-life care, so it was difficult to know. When he passed away, my

family experienced a great loss. But in some ways, we were also relieved, because those two years had been difficult and painful for my grandfather. Often, now when I think of my grandfather and his final years, I think of that window in his nursing home room. And I think about how as a family, we were in many ways unprepared to face the end of my grandfather's life.

Rebekah clearly had some experience here. Later in the message, she wrote the following broad historical context, and included logical evidence:

At the heart of this public policy discussion was the fact that our nation is growing older. People are living longer. In 1900, life expectancy in the U.S. was forty-seven years. Now it's on average seventy-seven years. In 2030, there will be over one million centenarians in the United States. No wonder we are wondering how will we best take care of our elderly.

Medicare was enacted in the 1960s as a major step toward a national contract to care for older Americans. At first the program was relatively small. In the course of our lifetimes, however, it has grown and evolved to represent one of the federal government's largest expenditures . . . currently over $200 billion annually.

Because there are more of us, and because we are spending more on each person, these expenditures are growing, and are expected to escalate to 10 percent of our GDP by 2070. They are currently just over 2 percent. Imagine, when we are old, one in ten dollars of our entire GDP will be spent to keep us alive.

Eugene Steuerle is a senior fellow at the Urban Institute, a Washington-D.C.-based think tank. He is an economist who has spent his life studying and writing about social issues and fiscal problems . . . both as an academic and as an executive in the Treasury Department. In a testimony before a Senate committee considering the fiscal implication of an aging population, Dr. Steuerle put forth the following:

"Every once in a while I wake up from a dream where a researcher from the NIH comes running into a hearing and proclaims, 'Eureka, I've found a cure for cancer.' Rather than celebrating and jumping up and down with glee, the members of the committee instead beat their brows and begin to commiserate among themselves. 'What is going on here? What is their problem?' I ask myself. Then suddenly I realize that they can see only the effect of the new medical miracle on the budget: higher health care costs and higher Social Security costs associated with longer lives."

Indeed, it is a good dilemma that we have, but it is a dilemma.[7]

This context has it all. We know the history of the issue from the standpoint of someone who has a competent association with the problem. We have numbers, we have an authority, we know the greater meaning of the issue, and we have the personal motivation of our leader. It would be easy to get committed to this issue, and easy to follow such a competent and personally engaged person.

Presenting logical support for change is an essential part of leadership communication. We respect leaders who have the facts in hand, but those who rely *only* on mental evidence to support their positions are often judged to be uncaring technocrats. Conversely, those who rely solely on emotional appeal and conviction are considered "more real." Both of these judgments are inaccurate. We are all blessed with the ability to reason and the capacity to feel, and it is the integration of these two faculties that is authentic. Leaders who can communicate both logic and passion are deploying themselves fully. Establishing a shared context is the core of a leadership message for change. Compose it well, and you will be prepared to communicate effectively and completely.

Questions to Ask in Creating Shared Context

Common Understanding of History

- What is the history of this issue? Where have we been?
- What has changed to make this issue timely or critical?
- In light of this history, why do we need this change now?
- Where do we currently stand?

Broader View

- What are the larger implications of this change?
- What broad opportunities or barriers stand before us in executing this change?
- Why should this be a priority in light of other important issues and priorities?
- Is the change I am advocating the best alternative?

Competence and Trust

- How can I reinforce my personal competence and trustworthiness?
- How can I establish myself as a leader rather than a mere carrier of information?
- Where was I in the context?
- How was I affected personally by the changes in history?

8

Declare and Describe the Future

As a young man, I was intensely interested in the relationship between prophecy and the future. Was the prophet predicting the future or creating it? The longer I live, the more I witness, the greater my conviction that the prophet is the visionary who imagines a desirable future and then declares it to the rest of the world. The declaration itself makes something seem possible that formerly seemed impossible. In declaring the possible, the prophet moves people in the direction of making positive change. Leaders do this same work. They declare the future and they describe it in a way that is compelling to others.

Declaration: An Act of Creation

In the early 1980s, when the cold war was at its zenith, Tom Green (my business partner) and I became enthralled by the application of this idea to the realm of international politics. Could leaders, imbued with enough power and imagination, begin the creation of a future that was beyond the current imagination of others, even across national and cultural lines? Could such leaders accomplish this with declaration? Research seemed to suggest that it could indeed be so. The Reformation, the creation of the United States, the freeing of slaves in America and later the American trip to the moon—these and other great shifts in culture or accomplishments of great goals were first conceived by and then given voice by a leader.

This insight led Tom and me to some intense, voluntary involvement with corporate and political leaders to suggest that the declaration of leaders could play a central role in shifting the perception of the world regarding the arms race. The available examples suggested that the greater the change desired and the greater the perceived power of the leader, the more likely that the change could actually occur. Tom and I were clear that if he or I declared the end of the cold war, no one would notice. What was needed was the conviction and declaration of change by leaders of the most powerful nations on earth, and the work of our small consortium centered on moving this idea forward.

Ronald Reagan and Mikhail Gorbachev stepped into this historic opportunity in 1985. When they met for a hasty summit in Reykjavik, Iceland, these two men were perceived by the world to have power over the fate of the arms race; indeed, perhaps over the fate of the earth.

The Reykjavik summit was known for a time as the "do-nothing" summit. No great agreements were signed, none were reached. But the end of the summit did not produce conventional rhetoric. Rather, both leaders declared that the world would never be the same. Here are their comments, quoted in the *New York Times*:

Reagan: "Mr. Gorbachev and I got awfully close to historic agreements in the arms reduction process. We took discussions into areas where they have never been before."

Gorbachev: "This was an important event. It has been a reassessment and has created a qualitatively new situation. And nobody is now in a position to act the way he was able to act before."[1]

Gorbachev's words were prophetic: "a reassessment . . . has *created*." He did not say "a reassessment has *predicted*." The power of these statements, the declaration by both leaders of the dawning of a new way of perceiving things, created the road to the end of the arms race. Shortly after this meeting, after years of necessary but apparently fruitless negotiation, the details of the Intermediate Range Missile Agreement were worked out . . . the first missiles were destroyed, and the world will never again be the same. One could certainly argue the merits of the outcome, but this change occurred almost as the German philosopher Schopenhauer has been paraphrased: *All truth passes through three stages. First it is ridiculed. Second it is violently opposed. Third it is accepted as being self-evident.* "New truth," to be recognized at all, has to be declared. This starts the process from ridicule to opposition to acceptance.

Most of us don't perceive ourselves as having the power to affect the fate of the earth, but each of us can inspire progress in some arena, even if it is only in our own lives. The leader who is formulating and advocating change is like Oscar Wilde's visionary: "a dreamer . . . one who can find his way by moonlight, and see the dawn before the rest of the world."[2] The leader is the young Parsifal, returning from his quest with a boon, but he has now told us that we must follow him, must change our ways and put ourselves at risk, in order to enjoy the future as it could be. The leader now needs to be able to describe the dawn to those who can't see it, those who reside in the dark. What will we see when the sun comes up? What will our world look like when we have completed the change?

Making it Real: Include Others in the Possibilities

Any change message has to include a description of the new world that excites the leader, so that the leader can excite others. This is not the place to dwell on the means, it is the place to focus on the eventual result of the combined effort. Neither is it a time to dwell on the hardship of the journey, it is rather a time to see the beauty of the destination. Obviously, the new future is a result of actions that the group might take, but the mere description of the actions themselves will not move others to act.

Antoine de Saint-Exupéry extolled: "If you want to build a ship, don't drum up the men to gather wood, divide the work and give orders. Instead, teach them to yearn for the vast and endless sea. As for the future, your task is not to foresee it, but to enable it."[3]

In Chapter Five, I discussed the power of analogy and metaphor, story, and personal experience to create and sustain culture and to inspire others to want to struggle together for a desired future state. Stories of the past and present provide evidence of need. Stories of the future provide a magnet to satisfy that need through change. To be committed, others have to see themselves in a movie-like image, playing a part in a story that is compelling, moving toward a state or objective that is more interesting and desirable than the status quo. The same is true for you.

To do this, to describe the future in a way that you and others see and feel it, requires an act of the imagination. It requires the talent, capability, and curiosity of the fiction writer. Seeing and feeling yourself visually and viscerally in the changed state is a powerful draw toward moving to that state. Whether it's called "affirmation," "positive thinking," "prophecy," "visioning," or "strategy," it is a way to *create* the future rather than *predict* it.

Walt Disney was the most imaginative entrepreneur of our time, and he had more than an intellectual understanding of this phenomenon of how the future gets created. Stories abound about his focused and creative genius. One concerned the building of Disney World in the swamps of Central Florida. The first phase, the Disney theme park, was completed in the early 1970s, and like Disneyland, at the center of what was then Disney World was the castle of Fantasy Land.

The original plan called for the park to be built from the outside in, with the Castle as the last piece of construction. But when Disney was about to give full approval to go ahead, he insisted on the Castle being built first rather than last, as a way of inspiring all of those who worked on the project. The Castle was the symbol of the future, the creation of yet another "happiest place on earth," an inspiring monument that would keep focus and meaning on the work at hand.

This same futuristic and imaginative characteristic is present in every effective leadership communication. More important, it exists in the imagination of the leader long before it is committed to others. Listen to Henry Ford's audacious declaration, in 1903, of the future of the automobile:

> I will build a motor car for the great multitude. . . . It will be so low in price that no man making a good salary will be unable to own one . . . and enjoy with the family the blessing of hours of pleasure in God's great open spaces. . . . When I'm through, everyone will be able to afford one, and everyone will have one. The horse will disappear from the highways, the automobile will be taken for granted. . . . [and we will] give a large number of men employment at good wages.[4]

Consider that this comment was made when the horse was the primary means of transport, there was very little infrastructure to support the automobile, and in fact, the motor car was thought to be only a novelty. Ford's commentary was an act of communication courage that inspired others to work toward the future he described. The result was not just the Ford Motor Company but a new way of manufacturing that transformed much of American industry.

If you can't envision a future that is compelling, you can't lead. You simply won't know where you are going.

Let's see how others have seen the future of change and documented it. John Ure of Agilent envisioned the future of his factory after the supply chain changes were made:

> I see the firehose neatly coiled on its rack. I see Marketing out of the factory having lunch with the customers, concentrating on understanding the market for new business rather than pacifying angry customers. I see the Manufacturing Head leisurely walking around encouraging others rather than frantically adjusting work patterns and machine loadings to cater for the products he doesn't have parts to make. I see operators chatting cheerfully as they work, with parts arriving at their workstation just when they need them, keeping the work

places clear, with evident pride. I see an empty rework workbench. I see no need for overtime to catch up, but a need for overtime to meet a last-minute new order generated by the customers' delight at the way we just dug them out of a hole generated by our competitor's inability to ship. I see a Quality department with no need to spend time checking up on parts as they come into the factory. Indeed, Quality can focus on adding value to the product through working with the design teams rather than adding cost by throwing away bad parts. I see suppliers who are successful in their own right, with capacity to exceed our demands. I see design engineers who only have to draw components once. Finally, I see a room full of shareholders giving a standing ovation to the board of the company, who have just delivered the first-quarter earnings, bang on target.

Will John say it this way every time? Of course not. But the reflection on the future, the writing of the imaginary conditions, will allow him to communicate with others in a way that can be compelling. More important, it gives him a clear target, a sensory-rich set of thoughts and feelings that will keep him inspired and keep him communicating about the possibilities in the change that he is advocating.

Highlighting the Intrinsic and Personal Value

Rebekah Saul Butler envisioned a future in which end-of-life conversations among families would be commonplace:

When I envision the future, I think of how this conversation would become a common and natural one among families all over the country. I'm imagining how it would play out while a family is on its annual summer vacation to visit the grandparents. One night, the grandparents and their children are sitting around the living room after dinner, with the smell of pot roast and cornbread lingering in the air. Someone, perhaps the grandmother, brings it up: "We're getting older, you know," she ventures. "It's about time for us to start thinking about our futures." The family would discuss the grandparents' financial security and housing options. And they would talk about decision-making protocols around health-care treatment; seeing a lawyer to put in place some legal mechanisms such as Advance Directives. In the course of the conversation, the grandparents would each share their own values around dying. Then, years later, in the case of a life-threatening medical emergency, the family would be able to draw upon these conversations. I'm imagining this family in a hospital, approached by a physician who explains the dire state of the grandparent's health. The family recalls previous discussions, reviews legal documents, and considers options in light of values that are well understood. I don't think that end-of-life conversations—and the decisions that go along with them—will ever be easy, but they will be easier, and more fruitful, if we have had conversations earlier in life as well as at these critical moments.

This kind of personal vision is especially effective, as it gives us the direct impact of the change on our own lives. Reflecting on your own experience of how it could have been different for you is a particularly effective way of thinking about it; a particularly effective way of communicating the benefits to others. Most of us can see ourselves in Rebekah's future, either having the conversation with our parents or having the conversation about ourselves with our own children.

The Stakes: Best Case, Worst Case

It is difficult for many change agents to envision the conditions that will exist if changes are made. They merely have this vague feeling that things will be better. But many times they can better envision what will exist if the changes are *not* made. Recording both the best case and the worst case is frequently as stimulating to a leader as only seeing the bright future. In fact, much of the time, it more than doubles the impact to communicate both possibilities. In his September 2002 speech to the United Nations regarding the Iraqi situation, U.S. President Bush related both:

> Events can turn in one of two ways. If we fail to act in the face of danger, the people of Iraq will continue to live in brutal submission. The regime will have new power to bully and dominate and conquer its neighbors, condemning the Middle East to more years of bloodshed and fear. . . . [But] if we meet our responsibilities, if we overcome this danger, we can arrive at a very different future. The people of Iraq can shake off their captivity. They can one day join a democratic Afghanistan and a democratic Palestine, inspiring reforms throughout the Muslim world. These nations can show by their example that honest government, and respect for women, and the great Islamic tradition of learning can triumph in the Middle East and beyond.[5]

Although these words were fashioned into a speech, the thinking of these two possibilities went on before the event, and the president's message platform now included these two scenarios. He referred to both in his drive to correct what he saw as a dangerous situation in Iraq: a future that is compelling *and* a future that is frightening.

In similar fashion, when Josie Gaillard was an MBA candidate, she developed the following message to communicate her belief in U.S. independence from foreign oil supply, envisioning and recording her alternate futures:

> If we continue to depend on foreign oil, I can promise you a future of oil shocks and recessions, poor Middle East relations and continued threats of terrorism. Families like mine will continue to live in fear of recession, in fear of the day OPEC members decide to raise oil prices and send our economy into

a tailspin. Children will continue to wonder why those angry people on the news hate us so much. Those same children will stay awake at night wondering when the next hijacked plane is going to fly into a nuclear power plant near their homes.

Now imagine a world in which the U.S. economy grows and prospers, unaffected by foreign oil prices. Imagine a world in which the U.S. is perceived as a neutral player, objective in its support of forward-looking nations and regimes while distancing itself from corrupt or repressive regimes in the Middle East. If we can reduce or eliminate our dependence on foreign oil by developing alternative technologies, I see a future of economic independence and greater objectivity in our foreign policy. This future will indeed bring peace and prosperity to you and me.

Of course, injustices are everywhere, and many issues need to be addressed and corrected. Some seem small; most seem daunting in their complexity. And each of these issues has many potential champions, most of whom don't know they possess the power, and many of whom don't care. Most people complain, a few get involved, and a very select few discover their own power to declare possibility and then create it through language.

What is it that excites you about the result of the change that you want to make? What will the world look and feel like when you have been successful? Announcing the possibility and then describing that world in sensory-rich terms will not only excite you and inspire others you speak to, it will actually begin the change process to make it real.

Questions to Ask in Declaring and Describing the Future

Declaration

- What new reality will be created with the change?

Making It Real

- What will our world look like when we have completed the change?
- What rich description can I provide for what it will look like when we have completed the change?

Stakes

- What are the intrinsically valuable and intangible benefits of acting on this change?
- What would be the consequences (tangible and intangible) of not taking action?
- How would it violate our values to avoid acting?

Values

- How will we be affected on a personal level if we don't act?
- What makes the change personally worthwhile, even though it might be painful?
- What value will be affirmed by the change?

9
___

Commit to Action

Leading out loud culminates in action. As you are nearing completion of the development of your message and begin to see the possibility of a new future, you also begin to see the first steps you need to take along the path. Some are general and organizational, others are deeply personal, and still others must be taken by those you want to inspire.

___

Organizational Steps Toward the Change

Thinking through the broad steps that the organization, institution, or company needs to take to move from the status quo to the new future helps you imagine the outcome, and it also helps your constituents see their roles more clearly. The greater the change, the greater the need to break things down into steps people can picture themselves taking. Consider what it took to go from imagining someone on the moon to those first steps on the surface of the moon. In tackling that mission, the U.S. lunar program was broken down into a chart of tasks which would lead to the goal. The first chart was far from complete. In several boxes representing the early steps in the project, the description read, "technological breakthrough needed here." Yet despite the obvious holes, thinking through the critical project benchmarks made a difference in the energy available for its accomplishments. So it is with smaller-scale change. Steps help to move others toward an outcome, down a logical path.

In contemplating the need for the United States to get free of dependence on foreign sources of oil, Josie Gaillard might write the following:

> This is a large problem which requires a steady commitment over years, but here are the fundamental steps we have to take as a nation. First we have to convince our leaders to declare this goal of independence as a priority in a fixed time frame in order to engage the imagination of the nation. Second, we have to revise our tax policy to encourage the development of alternative energy sources. This will fuel the innovative spirit of those who have the engineering ability to find substitutes for our substantial appetite. Some of these, if not most of them, are in the oil business today. Finally, we have to begin to convert the industries and products that use the greatest amounts of fossil fuels. Automobile engines are first, industrial facilities are next, and power plants not far behind.

These are the institutional action plans that will give others the guidance they need to plug their own talents into the process.

Similarly, John Ure needed to lay out the map to convert his supply chain emphasis:

> First, we need to develop together a comprehensive plan, to establish the priorities for me to work on, both with my teams and wherever I can be of added value. Second, we need to change the strategy with some of our critical suppliers, from pricing based on volume through forecasting to delivery. Finally, we need to assess the way we apply resources, and adjust that method to be consistent with our end goal.

These statements mark the clear path for the organization and stimulate others to find their place in the plan. They also set the stage for the leader to make a personal commitment, to take direct action as a way of getting movement started. Ultimately, it is this personal commitment of the leader that will inspire others to move, even as it is easier to continue to plan, to continue to discuss.

Personal Commitment, Personal Action

In his meticulous study, *Authentic Leadership: Courage in Action*, Robert Terry analyzes historic definitions of leadership and concludes: "If there is one dominant connection . . . it is action."[1] The leader can observe, contemplate, study and speak, but change only happens with action. Action is what we hear about, because without it, the message means nothing.

"I can attack with three divisions in the morning." These were the words of General George Patton in 1945 when Eisenhower asked a group of generals how long it would take each of them to be ready for an assault on Berlin. Because of this crisp and dramatic response—and his superiors' confidence in Patton's readiness—he was given the plum assignment of the campaign, the one that he believed to be the culmination of his life as a warrior.

Personal action is simple and eloquent, it sets possibility in motion, as I've learned many times in my own life.

In 1989, I ran across the United States with eighteen other people in "Transcon 89." The race was staged to raise awareness and money for a drug and alcohol prevention program in California. Each runner was responsible for about one and a half hours of running a day; and it was to be a race against time, not other teams. Only one other official attempt had been made to do this run, in 1986, and the record was more than sixteen days. Our team's goal was to break this record for the three thousand miles from San Francisco to the steps of the Capitol in Washington, D.C.

The leader of the group was Andy Mecca, director of drug and alcohol programs for the State of California. Andy is a dreamer, an inspiring leader, and of course a very accomplished amateur athlete. Under his leadership, a small group of us had planned the event for a year, honing the message, raising money, recruiting our team, and arranging logistics.

We left San Francisco on September 11, 1989, at 6 A.M. I was privileged to be in the group of four with Andy, and we spent the time when we weren't running in the same motor home, grabbing whatever sleep we could, eating as much as possible, and moving to our next rendezvous.

We ran night and day on Highway 50, moving across Colorado, Kansas, and into the Midwest. We crossed the Mississippi at Hannibal, Missouri, the night before a hurricane raked the southern coast of the United States, and made it into the rolling countryside of Illinois, through Indiana and Ohio. We touched West Virginia, and the day before we were due to arrive in Washington, our team ran the baton into Virginia, turned it over to the next team of four, and drove to the next rendezvous point.

We were scheduled to take the baton at 2 A.M. the same day we were to enter the District of Columbia and finish the race, but found ourselves parked and waiting on an access road for commuters into the city, a narrow two-lane road with ruts in the soft shoulders made by the eighteen-wheelers that had to move to the side to allow oncoming traffic to pass. It was raining hard and the wind was coming out of the east directly into our face. The wipers on the motor home had no chance to keep up.

For the first time on the trip, it felt like the continuity of the relay was in danger. We had managed to glean great cooperation from law enforcement all the way, but to control traffic on this stretch of highway, this close to D.C., was impossible. We were stopped at a turnout waiting for the runner to approach from behind, talking to our contact in Washington who was advising us to wait three hours until daybreak to continue.

Clearly, it was unsafe to do otherwise, but the run had not stopped for fourteen days. The spirit was high, the Navy chorus would be waiting at the Capitol along with many of the California congressional party. Pennsylvania Avenue was to be closed for us at the appropriate time.

ur of us were discussing the pros and cons as rain pelted the van, the wind moved the vehicle slightly from side to side as we saw the faint glow of the runner's flashlight appear in the rearview mirror, its bearer moving toward us for the exchange. In midsentence, Andy simply stepped out of the van and took the baton and started his reliable stride down the shoulder of the road. We had no choice but to follow in the van. He didn't relinquish the baton until daylight, when safety was assured. It was an elegant, inspiring, and decisive act of leadership that I will never forget. We set the record by nearly a day—fifteen days and one hour, for just over three thousand miles.

Could we have finished ahead of the old record anyway? Probably, but it would not have been a continuous run, and we would not really have reached our goal. We would have been compromised, knowing that it wasn't quite the same, and we would have wondered for the rest of our lives if we lacked the courage to reach our goal. Andy took the risk himself, and by doing so, made it possible for all of us to realize our dream of nearly two years. I'm sure in that moment before he stepped out, Andy knew that discussion would yield nothing, and that his action would galvanize the rest of us. I'm also sure that if need be, he would have run the baton all the way to the Capitol on his own.

The leader's commitment to action is the culminating and defining step of the change process. Critical as it is to know that the cause is important to you, to formulate your message so that it is clear and deep, to connect with the emotions of others, to define meaning, to create a shared context and to describe a future that is compelling, the final difference between the leader and others is a commitment to act. It is action that signals the victory of value over habit, of meaning over safety. It is a time when we are willing to stand for what is important. This action might be in firing someone, in closing doors, in compromising compensation, but it always speaks to the leader's commitment to the absolute need for change.

Accordingly, after describing the compelling future, your message has to conclude with a commitment to act. This section of your message is the most essential to write, and when you are writing it, you should feel as though you are at a threshold, perhaps about to open a door and look out into a void of sameness. Your decision is whether to step out or remain safely static. You will hear the voices in your head discussing your shortcomings, the severity of the risk you are about to take. You will be giving yourself advice like "I need another degree" or "I don't have enough experience" or "I need to take a workshop before I do this." These are just euphemisms for "I don't like looking out that door." Just as discovering what matters is an introspective process that brings forth values, the commitment to act will bring forth your fears—and ultimately, your conviction.

As you write this part of the message platform, consider the impact of the action you propose to take. Andy stepped out of the van on a rainy, windy dark morning. He could have said, "I'll tell you what, we'll wait here for an hour or so and see what happens." He could also have said, "Let's wait and talk to the others about it." Neither of these commitments would have inspired anyone, neither of them would display the courage of his convictions.

As you think about your commitment, picture it on an "impact" meter, similar to an applause meter. At the left side, the meter says, "I'll commit to call a meeting of others to discuss this further." At the right side of the meter it says, "I'll commit to put 100 percent of my bonus on the line. If we succeed, I get all of it; if we fail, I get none of it."

The difference is obvious, and the difference becomes even more obvious when it's not just money on the line. Consider the commitments of leaders who changed the world. Anwar Sadat went to speak to the Israeli Knesset, and doing so cost him his life. Martin Luther King Jr., Gandhi, Mandela each committed to act in nonviolent opposition to forces of oppression. They knew their message well, they delivered it well, and then they acted, with great risk of personal harm.

This principle has application in situations of far less significance.

After the Internet bubble burst in 2000, The Charles Schwab Corporation was facing severe layoffs in its ranks. The senior team met to consider their course of action. Without hesitation, the co-CEOs announced that their purpose was to keep as many people working as possible consistent with producing fair returns. They cut their own total pay by more than 90 percent for the year. Other officers followed suit, taking cuts from 50 percent to 15 percent depending on their relative position in the company. Each person took a pay cut in proportion to the opportunity they'd had to exceed their planned earnings in the boom period.

Only then did this team begin to consider what other cuts would have to be made. During the deliberations, employees volunteered to take pay cuts, to job-share, to take all of their vacations. They were inspired by the commitment to action shown by their leaders.

Other leaders we have been following in the text also made personal commitments that were inspiring. For example, in describing his commitment to the supply chain remedy he was proposing, John Ure made his own notes about his commitment and the cost to him personally:

> I intend to focus on our top ten suppliers to each business unit, travel around the world and visit them and any other elements in the chain in the next two months where my customers, you, the business units, feel this will help, and deliver the message you and I want them to hear. This might not sound like a chore; my five-month-old son thinks it is. He prefers me to tuck him in at night, and for me, every day away from him is like a year lying naked in an igloo. I plan to kick any stone out of the path that we agree on, and clear away any detritus I find hidden there. I do not plan to divert from this task until I hear you cry "Enough, we do not need or indeed want you anymore!"

John made this commitment even though he could have delegated it. His courage and commitment set the stage for him to ask others to come along—and for others to want to.

George W. Bush, addressing the nation several times in the wake of the September 11 attacks, made it clear that he was forging a new path, calling for a change in our practice, vowing a war on terrorism around the globe. At the end of his message to a joint session of congress and to the nation on September 20, 2001, he made his personal commitment very clear:

> And I will carry this. It is a police shield of a man named George Howard, who died at the World Trade Center trying to save others. It was given to me by his mom, Arlene, as a proud memorial to her son. This is my reminder of lives that ended, and a task that does not end. I will not forget this wound to our country, or those who inflicted it. I will not yield. . . . I will not rest. . . . I will not relent in waging this struggle for the freedom and security of the American people.[2]

The president's words gave us all the choice to make the same resolve. But the president didn't come to this conclusion to make a speech. He came to this kind of passion and commitment as he was considering his options and making his choice of how to lead the country. This personal commitment defined him for the terms he has in office, and at the time, it gave a nation the confidence that he could lead us forward.

Involving Others, Asking for Action

How can I involve others? This is yet another acid test, the step in message development that is most often skipped, even by the most convincing and passionate leaders. Somehow, many don't believe that it is their right to ask others to act, even on issues that define the group as a company, or the organization itself. The willingness to ask for action and expect it is an unmistakable attribute of leaders. It is their responsibility to spend the necessary contemplative time searching personal experience and reviewing the context to gain conviction about the human value of the proposal. It is their responsibility to do the necessary research to become convinced that the evidence supports the decision. Leaders must be willing to act personally to make the vision come to life. But finally, once heart and mind are in concert, it is the leaders' responsibility to clearly call for action on the part of those they are charged to lead.

It takes confidence to act on your own conviction. It takes real courage to ask another human being to do so. The action can be simple and easy to perform, but it must be definitive.

Frequently, a leader does not consider what action other individuals can actually take, and might be satisfied to propose only the organizational steps, a list of sweeping reforms that are far beyond the ability of any single person to effect. Individuals, however, become easily convinced that the issue is too large for their involvement; each person believes that "they" will handle the action, so "I" don't have to do anything. But the nature of commitment is that it is personal, and it requires an *act* of faith. Asking *only* for the implementation of a broad-scale and far-reaching agenda redirects the leader's remarks away from the individuals who now share the vision and toward that entity that has no power to commit. Leaders often address their requests to "the company," "the department," or "the state" in the name of seeing the big picture—calling for a list of reforms and unintentionally leaving others with the sense that the problem is just too big for them to act at all. A broad agenda may be appropriate, but if your message is complete and worthy, those who hear it and engage really *want* to be part of your vision, they want to be part of this new and exciting world you have called for. Asking for a simple, definitive action on their part will test the seal of your bargain, not an agreement to do as they are told, but an agreement to move down a path together. As they perform that simple act, they are affirming their agreement in principle with your proposition, and some level of confidence in your competence and trustworthiness.

John Ure's request was simple:

Obviously, I can't do this alone. I ask two things of you. First, lay to rest any ghosts you may have of what went before save to learn, and to motivate you toward a more delightful future. Please refrain from attaching blame for the past. Second, give positive feedback when you catch people doing things right. In fact, I ask you to come to me in seven days with twenty things that you have seen from people in this team where you have caught them doing things right. This will set us on our course.

As you might expect, Josie Gaillard's requests regarding gaining oil independence were simple and direct:

I would ask you to do one of these six things in the next month: Invest in a renewable energy mutual fund, buy power from a green energy provider instead of your local utility, trade your SUV for a convertible energy car, install at least one solar panel at home, write your congressperson about increasing federal emission standards, or tell ten friends why the U.S. addiction to oil must end.

It feels easy enough to do one of those six things, perhaps even two. Both John and Josie's requests were clearly stated, doable, and relatively easy.

Regardless of the gravity of the situation, offering personal action and asking others for their actions are essential and powerful parts of leadership communication. Boyd Clarke and Ron Crossland brought the following example to my attention.

In the spring of 1948 the leaders of the soon-to-be-born nation of Israel met. They knew the occupying British would soon leave their land and on the day after, eight neighboring states would start a war of annihilation. They needed money—lots of money. David Ben-Gurion, the leader at the time, asked his designated and professional fundraiser to go to the United States. Their goal: to raise another $20 million. "Impossible!" was the reply. "The Americans are tapped out."

Golda Meir, not a professional fundraiser but a leader of the Zionists, spoke up and asked to go. She had lived most of her life in Milwaukee and said, "These are my people." She was met at the airport by the director of the public relations firm that had been hired to help raise the money. The director asked to see her speech so he could edit it and coach her on its delivery. She told him she had no prepared speech, but felt strongly she would know exactly what to say when the time came. The public relations man held his breath as she walked onto the stage to address the Council of Jewish Federations, hoping she would not undo all he had been working toward. This is the speech she gave that day.

> Please believe me when I tell you that I have not come to the United States only because several hundred thousand Jews are in danger of being killed. That is not the issue. The issue is that if the Jews of Palestine survive, then the Jews of the world survive with them, and their freedom will be assured forever. But if these several hundred thousand are wiped off the face of the earth, then there will be no Jewish people as such and for centuries to come, all our hopes and dreams of a Jewish nation, a Jewish homeland, will be smashed.
>
> My friends, when I say we need money immediately, I don't mean next week: I mean right now. In less than four months, we will be fighting for our lives against cannon and armor. It is not for you to decide whether we will fight. That decision is taken: we will fight. We will pay for the birth of our nation with our blood. That is normal. The best among us will fall. That is certain. You can decide only one thing: whether we win or lose.[3]

Obviously, Golda Meir did not need to prepare a speech. She had developed her message over years of involvement and commitment. Everyone knew her competence, most trusted her. All the Jews listening knew the context of this issue: where they had been, where they were, and where they were going. The vision of a Jewish homeland had been shared for more than twenty years. Now it was time to act. Her own commitment was to die, to sacrifice her life. She asked them only for money—and she raised $50 million.

Your own message may not require life-or-death sacrifices, but if you want to lead change, you have to take action and request action.

Will everyone that you talk to act? Of course not. Many will squirm in their metaphorical seats and procrastinate. But keeping the request to act current will keep the engagement temperature at a point where others have to decide, and to finally commit, one way or another. To avoid asking for action is to avoid bringing others to the door of commitment, to avoid requiring that they choose. Some will act, and those who do will form the first wave of change.

Commitment to act, from the organization, from the leader, and from the community of individuals who will effect the change is the last substantive part of the leadership message. Once you have completed this part, you can begin to apply what you have developed in the myriad venues of leadership communication. In the next chapter, I will explore how the content you have developed serves as the grist for every leadership communication opportunity.

Questions to Ask in Committing to Action

Organizational Steps

- What steps does the organization need to take to effect the change?

Personal Commitment, Personal Action

- What personal commitment am I willing to make?
- What commitment am I willing to demonstrate with action?
- What specific action am I taking personally, irrespective of what others may do, that is significant enough to inspire others?

Involving Others

- What specific actions am I going to ask of others to give them a way to engage immediately?

10

Leadership Communication Applications

I'm hopeful that at least two things will have happened if you've followed the prescriptions in the first nine chapters. First, you will have recorded some values and experiences in a new way, and you will have extrapolated from those values and experiences one or two fundamental changes that are needed, changes for which you can take the lead. If you are new to the idea of yourself as a leader, it may have come as a surprise that you feel so strongly about something, or that you actually have the capability and interest to lead meaningful change in your family, your business or other organization, or in your community. If you are presently in a leadership position, then you have been able to record your change initiatives in a cogent and compelling form, one that is far removed from a briefing book or a white paper. Your message progresses from developing trust and displaying competence through giving and gaining commitment to action. You have been able to record all this as a platform for communication to others in a way that will inspire them.

The second outcome is that you have asked questions of yourself, and in that process of introspection you have expanded your awareness of the "other" in leadership, those you would like to inspire. You have seen leadership's requisites not only as a good idea, a drive to get results, and the competence to make decisions, but also as the ability to build relationships. With this insight, you might have seen the need to develop substantial emotional intelligence as a prerequisite to effective full-time leadership. You realize that with your change initiative now grounded in insight, personal experience, analogy and metaphor, story, and data, it's time for the next step, for this cause to get in stride with life itself. You need to begin communicating daily with the same awareness that you have displayed in the process of painstakingly developing the message.

These two outcomes are wonderful for me to imagine, and I know that their realization is no mean feat. It is one thing to be able to cite your ideas and feelings on paper; it is another to be able to communicate in real time, with some who don't agree, through the inevitable ups and downs of business cycles and other interruptions, through political crises and unexpected occurrences, through the predictable politics of support and withdrawal of support, the give-and-take, and the coming and going of fear and doubt—yours as well as others'.

I wish I could say that I know someone who does this impeccably. But I don't know any leaders who can always, without fail, muster the self-knowledge and control to put the cause before their own egos, who somehow always avoid the need for self-aggrandizement and hear others out, acknowledging good faith even when it might not be there; inspiring people to make progress toward a shared goal. I don't know anyone who can do that. In other words, I don't know any saints today.

Nonetheless, the goal must be eminent awareness and flawless execution. Armed with your message platform and with whatever emotional intelligence you can muster, you are ready to start communicating. The overarching goal of your communication is to inspire others to take action to effect change. The first objective of all leadership communication is to reinforce competence and trustworthiness.

If it seems a formidable and monumental task, remember that it can be broken down into steps, and each step can be practiced and improved. You first need to decide what medium to use, when to communicate, and how much to communicate. Possibilities range from the original declaration as a speech to the question period after it to informal conversations to ongoing communication (in a variety of media) about progress. Sometimes it is wise to deploy yourself personally and sometimes alternative channels of communication are acceptable, but the nature of the communication may differ in each case. Your preparation of the message platform will reap dividends regardless of the forum.

Change Message as a Speech

When a new possibility is declared, when the new reality is introduced, usually it's in a speech. It may not be as noteworthy as Kennedy's charge to go to the moon and back, but it will display many of the same elements. It might be a very public statement, like the Declaration of Independence. Or it could be more subtle, a simple message by a business leader to a small group at a retreat, a message that begins the transformation of a company. I've witnessed both public and more private moments and know that, whatever the forum and without fail, successful leaders who declare change do so only after a great deal of thought, introspection, and crafting, just as the process described in this book suggests.

Not surprisingly, leaders who take the time and energy to discover what matters, work for clarity, enhance their own emotional intelligence, and connect with others are able to speak with their authentic voice in prepared speeches; more so than even in spontaneous discussion. Composing a speech from your message platform gives you every opportunity to avoid arrogance and defensiveness and to display an attitude of confidence. As you compose, you can explore the history of the issue and look to your human experience for meaning. You can carefully scrutinize the evidence for truth and consult with others whom you respect. You can even rehearse your delivery, listening for the sound of authenticity, reworking where necessary to bring your Self forward. You also have the opportunity to talk while others listen—that is, until the end, when you are faced with the decision to solicit questions from your audience. It may seem logical and even authentic to do so, but in keeping with your objective to engage others, it is not always appropriate.

After the Speech: Is It Time for Engagement?

Even though maintaining trust requires that you to be willing to engage with others' questions, it is not always appropriate to take questions after a speech. The two primary considerations are the content of the speech and the size of the audience. If the speech is your first advocacy for a change, it is likely to be more abstract and less specific, written to inspire with context and values. Questions could prove frustrating for you and your listeners, and could drain away the excitement that your initial speech has generated. If your audience is large, taking questions is logistically difficult. The process needs to be tailored both to allow representative questions to be asked and to avoid ill feelings in someone not recognized due to time constraints.

In either case—if you're presenting to a big group or if it's your first declaration of a change—you should consider not taking questions. If these factors combine—you are delivering an abstract, value-based speech to a large audience—consider the compounded effect of these two negative influences and absolutely refrain from offering the audience a chance to ask questions. Imagine Dr. King finishing his "I Have a Dream" speech by asking for questions from the hundred thousand people massed in front of the Lincoln Memorial. Better that the audience members kept the power of King's words and delivery in their hearts as they shared their reactions to it with others in the crowd. Doing so allowed the speech time to take root.

Most of us, however, are not in situations like King's. More typically the size of audience and nature of material are not prohibitive, and in such cases you should *always* offer the audience the chance to clarify, contribute, or challenge your comments. When others can really participate, they are more likely to feel ownership and commitment. In offering to take questions, you are offering a direct relationship to *individuals*, in addition to the group as a whole. You build expectations of candor in the audience, and can greatly enhance or damage the credibility and trust you have constructed during the speech. Your success will depend on how you respond when the questions are finally asked—particularly the tough ones. If you can conduct the question-and-answer period displaying the same competence and connection that were obvious in your more formal remarks, you can further solidify the trust of the audience. Doing so requires tapping your emotional intelligence.

Listening and Responding with Emotional Intelligence

Emotional intelligence underlies the ability to relate to others. As noted in Chapter Four, emotional intelligence means knowing about emotions, recognizing them in yourself and others, being appropriately vulnerable, and making the goal of connecting with others more important than being right about the specifics. None of these objectives may arise naturally or immediately when you are questioned or challenged. Instead, each conversation could become a new battle to be won, each question a new threat to your cause and, more honestly, to your ego. In these moments, you forget that you are a leader and instead become a warrior, attacking with your passion, your authority, your position, and your command of the data. In your words and your stance, you dare anyone to say anything, and—they don't.

How can emotional intelligence help? By offering options that lead to inclusion instead of exclusion, and that create connection instead of opposition. The following pages set out guidelines for soliciting questions and responding to them after a speech, or in any other less-formal interchange. As you'll see, there are parallels to the guiding questions for developing the message itself.

Hear the Person, Not Merely the Question

William Miller, close friend and consultant, told me a story of working with an executive of a Texas company. This man was known as an autocrat, but he was exceptionally bright and extremely competent. To gain a benchmark for working with him, William suggested a 360-degree instrument that would solicit feedback from his direct reports. Before the feedback was complete, William asked the executive how he believed his subordinates would rate him as a listener. He responded, "I think they will say I'm a bad listener, but if you press them, they will say that I always get their content." The executive made this comment with the belief that his subordinates didn't understand what real listening was; that their response to the second question would somehow prove that he was effective.

He was exactly right in his prediction. What he didn't understand was that listening is not so much about data as it is about empathy and inspiration. "Did he get your content?" is a different question from "Did you feel heard?" The former deals with the mind, the latter with the emotions, and people will rarely trust someone who responds only to facts, never to them, leaving them to feel unimportant.

This Texas leader confused the need *to answer questions* with the need to *respond to people*. Yet anyone in a relationship has confronted this difference, and might have learned that both are necessary. Particularly when dealing with change or inspiration, responding to the person will lead to much better results, even if the question itself isn't answered with technical correctness.

In Chapter Six, I suggested that empathy—acknowledging others and acknowledging their points of view—was central to developing trust, and that trust has to be developed before commitment can take place. The same idea is true in soliciting and answering questions. Building trust is your first goal.

Solicit Questions Authentically: Be Aware of Your Internal Conversation

Unless you are speaking at a highly charged political rally, people listening to you will be reluctant to ask questions or make comments that will reveal their true objections. This is especially true when you have some authority, when others might fear putting themselves at risk in your presence. Most people will not call attention to themselves by being negative about a change, particularly after the first speech, or perhaps even for the first few months of a change effort. You must connect to get people to open up.

This skill may not be foremost in your mind after a speech. Instead, many leaders have a commentary similar to the following running in their brains: "Now I'm finished. I hope some idiot doesn't ask a stupid question or raise an objection in front of this group. Let's just get on with it. I don't want to have to prove my point over and over." It's unsaid, but it comes across nonetheless.

Even if questions are asked, convention allows all of us to evade the unpleasant. It is not comfortable to deal with anger, disappointment, or disagreement. It is tempting to treat questions and comments as though the intent of the commentator is stated only in the words. A leader will rarely be criticized for ignoring indirect challenges. Here is the unspoken bargain: the questioner hides the intent to avoid direct confrontation; the leader detects the illusion and ignores it to avoid dealing with the real issue. This is an insidious agreement. Authenticity demands that this bargain not be kept. The first to acknowledge the real agenda gains the respect and admiration of others.

Leaders who truly want commitment will solicit feedback in a way that frees people from those shackles of fear, knowing that each question or comment that is authentic will help free others who might otherwise not be willing to be heard. How do you do it? By having a different internal conversation, and then making it external. For example, if you were a leader standing in front of your constituents, you might be thinking these thoughts, saying these words:

> Now you've heard what I have to say and why I think this is the best way to change in order to get to where we want to go. I'm sure there are reservations, I would be amazed if there aren't some concerns about job security, whether your hours will change, how this change will affect you personally. I'm sure also that some of you disagree with this course of action. I've done the best I can, gotten the best advice, and thought this through thoroughly, but I'm not infallible, and there is still room for some adjustments for things we did not consider.
>
> I don't have all of the details worked out yet, and in fact I'm counting on all of you to help in that. That includes the asking of questions or the making of comments in this hall, right now, that will bring the real concerns to the surface. I'll do my best to respond.

Some of you might be thinking that expressing disagreement or insecurity would be an affront to me, and that you might be putting yourself in jeopardy. Some of you have perceived others in similar situations who suffered because of an ill-timed question. But we need commitment, not mere compliance with this change. Please ask questions or make comments that are real, so that we can move ahead with the course of action that is best for all of us. While it is best that we air as much as we can together, if you would rather not ask or comment in this forum, or if you think of something after we leave, or if we just don't have time to take all of your thoughts here, I invite you to use my e-mail box or just come and see me.

This is the same introspective process you used in developing the message: acknowledging resistance and showing your motivation and vulnerability. It develops trust, and takes the conversation to a new level of resonance. The first time you make these comments, you might draw some skeptics. But if you persevere, others will start to contribute. This kind of honesty fosters commitment.

Whether another's question or comment is made immediately after a speech or as part of another interaction, how you respond also demands emotional intelligence.

Responding Authentically to Both Question and Intent

Most questions are really two questions: the stated one that is literal, and the unstated one that is only pointed to by the words or emphases in the comment or question. Your first task is to discern when the stated and the unstated questions coincide and when they don't. Your second task is to respond to both. In doing so, you display competence and can generate a new level of trust.

The stated question is obvious; the unstated one may only be revealed in the subtleties of the voice, body posture, and attitude of the questioner. The former is the objective question; the latter is the intent of the questioner. Although they can be congruent, in cases of disagreement they rarely are.

Each question carries with it the background and knowledge of the questioner and the context of the speech itself. As you learn to be more discerning under the spotlight of questions, it can be helpful to think about questions in categories: contributions, requests for clarification, and disputes or challenges.

Contributions may be voiced as questions, but they're really comments of support. The "questioner" wants to be heard as sympathetic (the unstated intent) and elects to elaborate on the positive nature of one of the points of your speech by giving additional evidence or examples. If you agree that the example or experience of the questioner is appropriate, such contributions are easy to handle.

Questions for information and clarification are also easy to respond to. The stated and unstated questions are the same, and there are generally no negative feelings associated with the question. The questioner merely missed a point or wants some clarification about what you said.

You can handle contributions and requests for information easily by acknowledging the question, commenting or clarifying, and confirming that you have been responsive. These three steps are fundamental in responding to every inquiry.

But many questions or comments rendered in change processes are neither contributions nor requests for clarification. They are *disputes, challenges, or concerns*, and are often disguised in the rhetorical clothes of the other categories. The stated and unstated questions are not the same. For example, "I was having trouble hearing you from the back of the room. I believe you said that the company would save $4 million in the first year of this change. Is that the correct number?" *could* be a simple request for clarification—depending on how it's said. Or it might be rephrased as "I believe you said that the company would save $4 million in the first year of this change, but *I couldn't believe my ears*. Is that the correct number?" This brings the dispute to the foreground and is clearly something more. Whether the message is literal or conveyed subtly, it requires a different response.

"How many people will relocate to Detroit to accomplish the transfer of work?" is a request for more information. "How many people will *have to move* to Detroit to accomplish the transfer of work?" might carry disenchantment with the request. The changes in wording or even in energy signal a change in the intent of the question. It's quite possible that the questioner would make the intent less obvious—perhaps using the original, neutral words, but in a voice full of cynicism. Perhaps the questioner is sitting back, arms folded. But is that out of defiance or physical chill? Here's where all your powers of observation and emotional intelligence come into play. Disputes and challenges are rich in opportunity and risk. They call for maximum awareness and skill on the part of the speaker. Even the "body language" consultants can't give effective rules. You simply have to be aware of intent. Trust your intuition; it is usually correct.

Invested Listening: Inviting Support

As with developing the message itself, applying a simple framework to your responses to challenges can help you train yourself away from defensiveness and nonproductive communication. Defensiveness will erode trust. If you can find agreement with the questioner and respond to both the intent of the question and the feelings of the questioner, you can continue to earn the faith of others; you can make your communication productive. Once you become really invested in hearing the intent of the other person, you have a chance of gaining agreement and even commitment. These are the five primary elements of the invested listening model:

- Answering the stated and unstated question.
- Acknowledging feelings.
- Finding common intent.
- Distinguishing between your context, or point of view, and the questioner's point of view.
- Checking in: making sure that you have been responsive.

Listening perceptively to your constituents and discovering what's underlying their stated comments is important. But you need to respond in a way that connects with your listeners and shows them that you have truly heard them. By acknowledging their common intent, their concerns and their context in addition to their stated comments, you can build an environment for trust and openness. You also open the possibility for further innovation related to the change, since your constituents may indeed have ideas and insights, based on their unique experience, that would improve the effectiveness of the plan you are suggesting. Your challenge is to balance inquiry with advocacy. You have to convey not only that you are open to input about how to achieve results but also that you are committed to moving the vision forward.

At a conference on illegal drug use in New York in 1994, the primary speaker advocated spending more federal money on drug treatment services. She entertained a "question" from a listener who immediately agreed with the speaker's context and went on to suggest the abolition of the federal drug enforcement effort. The "questioner" finished with an endorsement of drug legalization.

The instinctive response would have been to defend against the subtle attack: "I don't believe that legalization is an answer to the drug problem. I think it is short-sighted, sends the wrong signal to the wrong population at the wrong time, and would kill far more of our young people than the current rash of drug violence." That answer might be technically correct from the speaker's point of view, but it is only responsive to the disagreement with the questioner. Had the speaker confirmed the common ground with the questioner (the context of the problem), acknowledged the feelings that were present (frustration and anger), and then made the distinction in their positions (legalization versus treatment) she could have maintained mutual respect and reinforced her own solution. For example:

I appreciate your support for an increase in our investment in treatment. But I also hear your deep dissatisfaction with the drug enforcement effort and our level of federal spending to support that activity. Your comments reflect the frustration of many who see drug crime continue to rise with an ever-increasing death toll among our young. I share that frustration.

While we seem to agree that increased treatment will have an impact on those already addicted, I believe it would be bad policy to signal our youth that illicit drugs in *any* quantity would be appropriate to use. I believe, in fact, that the enforcement effort over the years has been a holding action, effective at maintaining pressure on supply while we have been developing our understanding of demand reduction strategies. The next few years of a more *balanced* approach of supply and demand reduction should yield even better results.

This response emphasizes the area of agreement, acknowledges the feelings of the questioner, and still makes the distinction between the two positions. The key elements are first, speaking to the common ground and second, openly acknowledging the intensity and opinion of the questioner. Like openly acknowledging resistance in the beginning of a speech, these aspects of the "answer" can deepen the connection between the listener and questioner, and can signal a level of safety to the rest of those who hear the exchange, or who hear of the exchange later.

At a town hall meeting of two hundred senior managers in the southwestern United States, the popular, well-respected CEO was entertaining questions. He had spoken earlier about a bright future for the company and had implored everyone to look to both revenue enhancements and cost savings in their respective operation. This was a public company and the CEO's annual salary and bonuses had been posted in the paper the previous week—in seven figures. The latest quarter's performance had been good, but not fantastic.

The question came from a field manager. The tone was very flat and noncommittal: "Uh, I have an employee who is the backbone of our operation. She comes in early in the morning, stays late at night, takes the initiative to solve customer problems and is the cheerleader for the rest of the office. Her job classification doesn't qualify her for stock options in our company. Now you make a lot of money, much more than I do, and . . . I'm sure you deserve it. What are we doing about passing the opportunity for options down to employees like her?"

As a consultant, I was seated in the back of the room calmly attending to the questions. Conversely, the CEO was seated on a stool on the stage with bright lights in his eyes. He was faced with responding in a cogent way while keeping up appearances. The *stated question* was a request for information: "Are we going to lower the requirements for employees to qualify for stock options?" The *unstated concern* was to call into question the pay scale of the executive. The *feelings* were resentment and probably some anger. The real question was a challenge: "Why do you make so much money when the rest of us do all of the work?" Unsophisticated, perhaps, or even immature, but real. At some level of consciousness, everyone in the room heard the real question.

The CEO launched into an answer to the stated question, reviewing the history of the option plan, reminding the audience of the many ways employees could gain ownership in the company, and explaining why the option plan was reserved for employees of a certain level. When he was finished, he asked the questioner if he had answered the question. The questioner said, "I guess so," and left it at that. This CEO did exactly what most of us would do, only he did it slightly better.

Later, I reviewed the meeting with the CEO. When I came to this question, I asked him if he had heard what *I* had heard. I played the question back from the recording, and he remembered the split second when he had heard everything: the words, the intent, and the feelings. In less time than we can measure, he had chosen his answer, following his underlying instinct to protect, defend, and justify.

We reviewed other possibilities, and decided on this one:

Tom has asked about our reasons for limiting stock options to directors and above, but I hear some other concerns in his question as well, concerns that go to the issue of execu- *(Respond to the stated question and the common intent.)*

tive compensation in relationship to the pay of others. In case I'm right about that, I want to respond to those issues as well. *(Acknowledge the feelings and unstated concerns.)*

First, on the issue of options. We have found over time that employees below a certain pay level use options only as compensation. They execute their options and cash them in right away. The purpose of any stock ownership plan is to encourage people who work in the company to have a real stake in the company's performance. So we think that the opportunities that we have to purchase stock in 401(K) programs accomplish that purpose. Above and beyond that, everyone can buy stock at a discount through the stock purchase plan, and there are no restrictions on how long you must hold that stock. Does that respond to that part of your question, Tom? *(Answer the stated question.)*

Now, to the larger issue of executive compensation, I want you to know that I appreciate anyone who cares enough about the company to be concerned about this, and I particularly admire his courage in asking *me* that question. He pointed out that the real heart of this company is in employees like the one he described, people like you who come to work in the branches every day and interface directly with our customers. I know and appreciate that as does every member of the executive team. If we aren't telling you that enough, then we need to get out more. *(Answer the unstated question.)*

The whole issue of executive compensation is the subject of much publicity right now, and Tom's question gives me a reason to speak to it directly. I have an interest, as you do, in making sure that our company is

spending its compensation dollars in the
best possible way.

As some of you know, executive com-
pensation is set by the board of directors, *(Distinguish*
specifically by a committee of outside direc- *between their*
tors. We set it up this way to avoid any ap- *context and*
pearance of being self-serving, and to assure *yours.)*
that we emphasize long-term results rather
than short-term movement in the stock
price. That means that the officers are paid
the bulk of their compensation on the basis
of long-term objectives and a smaller portion
on year-to-year operations. For a company
in our stage of development, that seems like
the right course to me.

The compensation committee also as-
sures that we are competitive in our industry,
so that the officers aren't moving to competitive firms because we were short-sighted.
In all the process seems correct, but it is certainly a process that is open for any of you to
inquire about further.

This morning, I talked about the need
for all of us to improve our revenue stream
and control costs. Those objectives are in
keeping with our plan for more long-term
investment next year in order to fuel what
we see as dramatic growth. At the end of our
five-year plan, I believe we will all see that the
investments we are making now in compensation will have been well-placed and that
they will result in greater opportunity for all
of us. I hope that is responsive to that issue, *(Check in.)*
Tom. And again, I appreciate your bring-
ing it up.

This was obviously easier to compose after the fact. We did not use it as a "revision" for the questioner. Rather, constructing this answer was part of coaching the CEO to respond more authentically the next time he was confronted with a similar situation. In contrast to the more leisurely development of the message itself, the question-and-answer session requires your attention in split seconds. Practice and review can provide you with the reminders you need to respond more effectively in the future.

Challenges and disputes, whether hidden and subtle or open and aggressive, present opportunities for new levels of engagement with the others. As you learn to listen (and observe) more attentively and intuitively to your own emotional responses and those of others, and as you invest the courage it takes to acknowledge what you hear (and see), you create an atmosphere of trust and openness. Using elements of the invested listening model will help you achieve interactions that are clearer and deeper, more connected and more candid. You will, as a result, get real engagement rather than mere lip service or conventional responses. Like the sequence suggested for message development, these steps act as a map toward an authentic response. Practicing them will make you more thoughtful, less defensive, and more responsive to others.

The Daily Practice of Leadership Communication

When people think of delivering a change message, a speech or presentation is the application that most often comes to mind. However, it is in the far more frequent informal and spontaneous conversations—in the town halls, small meetings, and one-on-one conversations that take place in conference rooms or offices—that leadership is most often practiced. Every time you write an e-mail message, discuss your initiative over coffee, do an interview with the press, or have an informal phone discussion, your message and your interest in engaging must come through. To be effective as a leader you must understand how to bring yourself authentically, in your real skin, to the full range of situations that will move your advocacy forward.

All of your communications are built on the foundation of core ideas that make up your leadership message. Who you are and what you care about does not change in the course of moving from a formal speaking event to a casual conversation—although finding the courage to express the reality of your human-ness may come more easily in one situation than in the other. In informal conversations and discussions, of course, all of this must happen in real time.

To gain support for a change, it's more important to create an environment in which people feel safe to honestly express real thoughts and feelings, including disagreements, than it is to deliver a speech with authenticity, clarity, and heart. Having made the decision to lead, you have a responsibility to extend yourself beyond your immediate emotional response to one that includes empathy for others regardless of the situation. This is not always easy. In fact, it is rarely easy. But if you are going to lead, it is essential.

Earlier in the book, I highlighted John Ure's change message for Agilent. With John's permission, I've included some scenarios in Appendix B that could have occurred as he tried to implement that change in the supply chain. The examples are purely fictional—and typical of what might have occurred had John not taken steps to move into authentic dialogue.

You will note that by recognizing his emotional reaction to any questions or challenges, John could move himself one step away from acting it out, through acknowledgment. As we learned with resistance, openly acknowledging a feeling defuses it and allows us to get to a deeper place, to get the feeling in perspective rather than reacting to it. From there, we can offer the truth, a logical and emotional response that is more complete, more authentic, without giving up any conviction. Such a response offers the opportunity to have a candid dialogue in which things that might otherwise be glossed over can be said.

Deploying the Self Proactively

In the process of change, communication is what fuels progress toward the new state. After a declaration, many informal conversations will occur. These are difficult, in that they can be spontaneous occurrences that catch you when you have other things on your mind.

But in addition to answering questions and having dialogue, a leader communicates proactively, purposely reminding others of the progress and lack of it, cheering and cajoling, measuring and asking for feedback. Much of this communication simply must be done in person. In Appendix B, I also discuss ongoing communication and the most critical of these forums: assessing the performance of others. These interactions are difficult to accomplish objectively while still responding to the emotional content. Accordingly, they simply have to be done in person. Almost every other kind of leadership communication can be done electronically, but only after you have earned the privilege—only after the recipients know you and trust you. Only then can recipients fill in any literal ambiguity from their personal experience of who you are. Whatever form these messages take, the key element is your deployment of your Self, your commitment to be satisfied only with inspiration rather than information.

In change efforts, proactive messages are critical to progress, as others are constantly reassessing, asking themselves: Why are we doing this? What is my role? Am I secure here or not? Do the leaders know what they are doing?

All this uncertainty can be allayed, but not with information alone. Rather than needing only rational explanations to commit, most people need emotional reinforcement. This is the leader's charge, to maintain a leadership perspective in all communication throughout the process, in every proactive change communication that takes place, even electronic communication.

Ross Dove is CEO of DoveBid, a California company that assembles disused industrial assets and auctions them off. Ross is an animated and thoughtful leader who communicates well, and often. He travels worldwide, visiting his more than seven hundred employees personally twice a year. Once a quarter, Ross drafts a Chairman's Letter and distributes it by e-mail to his entire company. If he did this every day, or even once a week, it's possible that no one would read it. But once a quarter, everyone looks forward to it. Notice the elements that he covers in this excerpt:

A Chairman's e-mail in mid-August . . . ugh. I'm fresh back from vacation and hope you are all having a great summer and have also enjoyed some time off. Like most of you, I don't realize how tired I get and how much I need to recharge my batteries until about the third day away from calls and e-mail. The good news is by about the seventh day, I can't wait to get back in the game because I don't think there is a job on earth more fun than this one.

After a dozen Chairman's letters, I thought I would give you all a break from vision 2010 and my "Knute Rockne" pump up speeches. Instead, I find myself in a more reflective mood and ask you to stop, take a breath, and spend a moment with me to enjoy what we have already accomplished together. Today, we have a company where many of us have become great friends and partners and just like my eighteen-year-old son says to his friends, "Don't worry, I've got your back," I believe a lot of us are beginning to feel exactly that. We can now count on, lean on, and trust each other to be loyal to the enterprise and the vision and to truly admit and acknowledge our success will come from every one of us doing our part and helping the next guy look and feel good.

Of course, the greatest challenge ahead is to set a high standard for that culture and live up to it. The greatest challenge I find personally is that with 700 people, every day I am bombarded with more and more information . . . good and bad. The bigger you are the more deals you win and ironically the more deals you lose. The bigger you are the more support and compliments you get as well as more criticism. One of the most interesting criticisms I have been receiving is that DoveBid is becoming too competitive internally. I have been told that there is a great deal of focus on salespeople competing with each other rather than with our competitors. That there is interdepartment competition for promotions and that some people believe all of this has raised a level of tension in our enterprise. It is a good criticism and one I will need your help with.

Simply stated, we win when our clients win and our clients win when they get the best possible representation from DoveBid. Each of us has different skill sets and we are stronger together. In all companies, this is a challenge and it cannot be resolved with rules. It must be resolved with the golden rule. If everybody comes together with the belief that ultimate equity comes from constantly striving to be fair then sound and good business judgment will always be the deciding factor. We all know the very best athletes are always gracious in both victory and defeat and they are really most passionate about effort. We all need to address this issue, and I know it can't be done by e-mail alone. So with a little luck, I'll be planning and executing two roadshows, one to the institutions, followed by an around-the-world trip to come see every one of you.

Ross starts by acknowledging the fact that some might find the letter long, then lets them know his motivation: it is a letter of gratitude. He introduces the problem of internal competition, tells a story of a similar situation (not included here), and suggests the solution. He then asks for their help and makes a commitment.

Because Ross travels extensively, because he provides every employee with some experience of knowing him, these employees view his e-mailed Chairman's Letters as notes from home. They know him. They know his intention and understand it. Ross has earned the right to communicate in this way by deploying himself personally. People in his company fill in the blanks of intention, even when Ross forgets, because he forgets so infrequently.

Electronic communication (voice mail, e-mail, video) to support your change efforts is only as effective as your ability to continue to deploy your Self as well as provide information. Regardless of the form a communication takes—a speech, a town hall meeting, an informal conversation, an e-mail message, or any other—your overriding responsibility as a leader is to be there, in the communication, rather than being beside it. Authenticity is the bridge from compliance to commitment, from satisfaction to loyalty, from mere change to progress. It is central to effective leadership in this new century.

Epilogue

The Cauldron of Leadership

It's an old adage. Put a frog in boiling water, it jumps out. Put the frog in water and increase the heat slowly, it will stay until cooked. So we have been about our need for real leadership. What I've suggested in these pages is that the practice of authentic leadership communication has been slowly waning, even as the need for it is becoming greater. With the erosion of authenticity, trust in our leaders continues to fade. We have become used to judging appearance rather than substance, yet as the world changes more and more swiftly, our need for grounding in reality becomes ever greater, our frustration with imitations more profound.

To effectively communicate as a leader of change in this new interdependent world will require a reversal of this trend, a defying of convention that has snared us in fantasy. Leading is about inspiring others to make change, and organizational leaders who foster joint commitment to meaningful endeavor will excel. Those who still depend on engendering passive compliance will falter. It is the energy of collective conviction that will fuel answers to the complex questions of global competition, national social malaise, fanatical extremism, and international cooperation.

People make commitments to causes they value and to people they respect and trust. Rediscovering an authentic voice and maintaining a commitment to meaningful change are requisites for any leader who would respond to these needs. Such authenticity requires speaking from both the mind and the heart, directly to the minds and hearts of the others. When those who listen sense both competence and connection, they are willing to engage, to consider their own commitment, and eventually to act.

Ideas can be learned from others, but passion lives in our own experience. The first step of creating change in any venue is to rediscover what is personally meaningful by reflecting on the actual shaping events of our lives. As leaders, increasing knowledge of internal truth must be a central theme in our lives, and will, as a discipline, tend to deepen all our messages. Perhaps that deepening can slake the technological thirst to make shallow messages more broadly heard. Technology can replace almost all parts of the body, but it cannot synthesize the whisper of the human spirit. By paying attention to those most important urgings, we can amplify that whisper to an audible call. Having thus reexperienced our own conviction, we can begin to bring it to others.

We've learned from history that all change starts from a stirring in some individual human soul. We also know that communication is the lifeblood of relationship. From the first word on paper (or the first utterance of wonder from your mouth) to a change being fully and finally manifested, you as leader can become a vehicle to carry others to decision and commitment. By including both facts and feelings, by exposing both credentials and personal qualities, and by entering into the interaction with others honestly and completely, you can offer real meaning in addition to the objective rewards of shared accomplishment.

Because we are out of practice at being real, because the veil of conventional, civilized behavior lies lightly upon us and is easily parted—particularly when the ideas and initiatives we value deeply are questioned or challenged—I have offered some frameworks that will encourage the use of both objective and subjective evidence, that will engage you as well as those you inspire. But because authenticity depends on your intent, the only guarantee of success will come from your own subscription to these ideas and your dedication to rekindling that intent each time you communicate, whatever the form.

I know from experience that consciousness doesn't come easy; it comes in hard-earned billionths of a second. But there are ways of training ourselves to expand those moments to full seconds, minutes, hours, and sometimes days. When we communicate authentically, we add immensely to the possibility for others to do the same, and for real leadership to once again emerge in the human family and to defeat cynicism one encounter at a time.

I realize too, that our world has made authenticity more frightening, even to the most stalwart of souls. There may be a price to pay in terms of ridicule by those who can't match your courage, but that is the price of leadership. Authentic does not mean indecisive. Vulnerable does not mean weak, and we need not abandon the mind to listen to the heart.

It takes work to remember that we are connected first as human beings, rather than only through our roles as professionals, capitalists, politicians, or students. In our lives of planning and executing, the reality of our human-ness and its inseparability from the parts we play rarely surfaces unless we make time and develop a discipline to see it. This book is meant to encourage you to take that time, to provide a discipline for you to use, and to implore you to actively and authentically communicate your discovery to others. Those you lead will be richer and more successful for it, as will you.

Appendix A

The Choice and Use of Evidence in Leadership Communication

In the introduction to Part One of the text, I stressed the point that leadership communication is both clear and deep. Because generally we are better at the clear part than the deep part, I've said little about evidence in the text. But following some principles of evidence can add immensely to the understanding and receptivity of others.

In Chapter Seven, I used an example by John Adams. The evidence he uses about the need for corporate emphasis on family issues was clear:

"Fewer than 22 percent of married-couple households consist of a male breadwinner and female homemaker. In the 1950s, the figure was 80 percent. Fifty-eight percent of mothers with children under six now hold paying jobs. The figure was 20 percent in 1960. And 68 percent of mothers with children under 18 work outside the home."

Roddick's evidence, also in Chapter Seven, was not as clear. "How bad is it?" "How many?" and "How much?" are questions that you have to ask yourself, and of course, are questions that will be on others' minds. Here are some guidelines to have your own evidence be heard more clearly.

Data: Specifics Encourage Engagement

We equate specificity with certainty, so precise evidence is far more powerful than generalities. When evidence is specific, it allows comparison and judgment, engaging others in a mental process rather than treating them as passive receptors.

Al Clausi, president of the Institute of Food Technologists, was an advocate for food research. As such, he had to develop a message platform that would engage his constituents. To support his advocacy, Clausi added a few specific pieces of information:

"Food is our nation's largest manufacturing sector. The annual value of shipments by the nation's 16,000 food manufacturers approaches $400 billion. Adding value to raw farm commodities, by processing them into foods, employs 1.5 million Americans. In 1991 we contributed $145 billion in 'added value' to our domestic economy. That compares with chemicals, including pharmaceutical, that contributed $155 billion, and transportation equipment, including cars, that contributed $152 billion."

Later, to support the need to promote health and safety in foods, he added: "If improved nutrition reduced health care costs by 10 percent . . . a realistic goal . . . the savings to the country would be $14.6 billion."[1]

This data was all specific, and therefore engaging and effective. The comparison of the food industry to other industries (drugs and cars) that were known by his constituents also provided a meaningful comparative for the statistics.

But what if Clausi had used only generalities, saying: "It is sufficient to say that the nation's food manufacturing sector is huge. It compares favorably with the chemical and transportation industries in its size and impact on American jobs and GDP." And later: "If improved nutrition reduced health care costs by a few percent, the results would be enormous."

It isn't hard to hear and feel the difference. Specificity enhances your credibility. It provides evidence that you have paid close attention to the issue, rather than merely reading a briefing book.

Relevance: Making Data Meaningful to Others

Frequently, the relationship of the data to others is not at all clear. In those cases, rather than letting them struggle with the relevance, you can tell them directly what it means.

At my younger son's university graduation, the chancellor took his obligatory turn at the microphone and used ten minutes to encourage our financial support of higher education. He used data to substantiate the excellence of the school, naming the number of Nobel Laureates on the faculty and the amount of research money they were able to attract. He used statistics, comparing the amount of research money procured by the university to like numbers from other top universities in the United States.

It was interesting but not engaging. As I surveyed the audience of students and parents with my speech critic's eye, I could see that the level of attention was due to the audience's pride in accomplishment, not because of any impressive thoughts or inspiring messages from the chancellor.

Finally, he remarked on the increased competition to gain admission to the university that had resulted from its enhanced reputation. He quoted the minimum combination of SAT score and grade point average required for admission four years previously, and compared it to the same standard today. It was much tougher to gain admission today than it had been in previous years. He then commented: "This means if you look to your left and your right, one of the two people you see, your fellow graduates, would not be admitted to this institution if they were applying today."

The atmosphere in the audience immediately changed. The chancellor had made it possible for each person to *experience directly the relevance of the data.* As I was listening and watching the students look right and left, I was also wondering if my son would have been one of those who would still gain admission. My mind immediately made the data *personal,* and as a result, I felt a much closer connection to the statistics, and a much closer connection to the speech.

Global Data Made Local

A third effective way of making contextual data relevant is to express it in terms of a familiar setting. If the evidence is global, or in a context that is not familiar to the audience, the numbers can be cast in a more commonplace background.

Timothy Wirth, who was quoted in Chapter Five, cited the following statistics about the loss of farmland in China: "And in China, home to one in five of the earth's people, severe water shortages and soil erosion threaten that nation's ability to sustain its population. Between 1957 and 1990, China lost nearly 70 million acres of cropland, *an area the size of all the farms in France, Germany, Denmark, and the Netherlands combined.*"

Wirth expressed the data in a setting (Northern Europe) that was more familiar than China to his audience. Given that his audience was made up exclusively of Americans, he could have been even more effective had he related the loss in China to a land area in the United States; for example, North Dakota, Nebraska, and Kansas.

Data is an essential part of the justification for change. However, it can be communicated in a way that includes others, encourages the interaction with them, and adds to their respect and trust for the leader.

Quotations from Authorities: Support for Ideas

As you develop your message, you will often quote an authority who agrees with your ideas as a way of adding weight to your evidence, and occasionally to deepen your connection with others. But done without reflection, it can also *damage* both aspects of your credibility. For example, it is a common mistake to quote a philosopher, academic, or other expert without really knowing whether the source's body of work bears out your point; or worse, to quote a person others don't know, leaving them wondering about their own intelligence. You can seem arrogant and aloof when this occurs.

Consider these references to authority in Timothy Wirth's speech. Again, his topic was "Sustainable Development," and his audience was the Washington Press Club and several thousand of the American public watching the speech on television. Referring to the danger of the increasing use of natural resources, Wirth said: "Professor Tad Homer-Dixon of the University of Toronto warns that in the coming decades, quote, 'resource scarcities will probably occur with a speed, complexity and magnitude unprecedented in history.'" Wirth went on, "Current conflicts offer a grim foreshadowing of Robert Kaplan's coming anarchy, the anarchy that could engulf more and more nations if we fail to act." These obscure references to Homer-Dixon and Kaplan damaged Wirth's credibility rather than supporting his case. He verbally stumbled over the references, and chances are very good that most of the audience had not heard of at least one of his authorities. How could he have made these references more authoritative and authentic?

First, by assuring his own familiarity with the authorities, and second, by explaining their credentials to the audience. For example: "Professor Tad Homer-Dixon of the University of Toronto is one of the world's authorities on environmental security. He has authored several widely read articles on how environmental problems can lead to conflict in developing countries, and was a keynote speaker at the U.N. conference on population and development in Cairo. Professor Homer-Dixon says, and I quote, 'resource scarcities will probably occur with a speed, complexity and magnitude unprecedented in history.'"

Wirth could have augmented his reference to Dr. Kaplan as well: "Current conflicts offer a grim foreshadowing of a coming anarchy that could engulf more and more nations if we fail to act, an anarchy foretold by Robert Kaplan in his recent frightening cover article in the *Atlantic Monthly*." By expanding these references, Wirth would have strengthened *his own* credentials and would have shown more respect for his audience.

Experts Who Are Real

It is possible to deepen the connection with others even further by relating your relationship with the "expert." Did you read the works of Bertrand Russell as a teenager growing up in the Bronx? Did your father talk to you about life on fall evenings on the porch in San Diego? Did you read every speech that John F. Kennedy ever delivered? Did you study Zen koans at a temple in Kyoto? Explaining the source of your respect for the authority deepens the level of intimacy with others, adding to your credibility and your humanity, encouraging their engagement with you and the change you are advocating.

Many of the greatest lessons I have learned have come from people who are close to me and who have gained their expertise through *experience*. When I quote these people, I am also sharing a part of my life with the audience; and they sense the authenticity in that sharing. For example, I know a woman minister who began attending seminary in her late thirties. She had been successful in business for the preceding fifteen years, but had been unhappy with what she perceived as a constant moral dilemma. The decision to give up her career was not easy. She asked everyone she trusted for advice, prayed about her decision every day, even sought professional counseling on the issue, but could not gather the courage to make a decision. Finally, at an evening meeting at the church, she announced that despite a severe shortage of resources and not having a place to live, she was going to leave her job and enroll in seminary for the fall term.

A month later, this woman was back at the church for the same group meeting. By then she had secured a scholarship and a place in the student housing center. All the resources she needed had become available as soon as she had made her decision. That second night she told us, "I always thought that I needed clarity to create commitment, but now I realize that it is the other way around—it is commitment that creates clarity!"

I use this story as evidence whenever I discuss the power of commitment. It never fails to connect me with others and to add a great deal of authority to my remarks. The quotation is not merely an abstraction that I read in some book. The power of the quotation is both in the words, which may be seen as universally true, and in the obvious impact on me, the advocate. Other people appreciate the intimacy inherent in quoting someone I know personally. I was there, the woman was real to me, and that reality gets transmitted to the audience.

Authentic leaders collect the writings and sayings of those people who have actually had an impact on their own lives, not the most popular people or even the most noted authorities (although these categories can overlap on the personal impact group). When they quote such authorities, they also include the circumstances of discovering the citation. Such authenticity adds immeasurably to the power of the supplemental authority.

Applying these rules of evidence will enhance the clarity of your message to others, making it more relevant and meaningful, and adding to their recognition of your competence and empathy.

Appendix B

Expanded Applications

Soliciting and answering questions and generating proactive communication through other media are common to leaders of change, and were covered in the text. These situations lend themselves to practice, models, and rules. In many ways, the leader can observe these situations, reflect, and react appropriately. More difficult are the casual conversations that include some objection, emotional or logical, to the change; or the actual performance appraisal, the communication that the leader has to institute to assess progress of individuals and inspire them to do better or more. This appendix will comment on both these situations as a way of bringing them to consciousness and facilitating more fruitful outcomes.

Follow-Up Conversations

Since you are familiar with John Ure's situation, I've created some fictional scenarios—things that might have happened when he talked with the people he is counting on for support in implementing his changes. John's advocacy for a change in Agilent's supply chain is eloquently and authentically expressed in his message platform. When thinking about resistance, he identifies how the design department will likely react to his ideas (*"Don't come and tell me how to design a product."*) In a follow-up conversation, the head of the Design group *might* respond by saying something along these lines: "Look, if you want to spend your time dealing with customer service, take it over to Marketing. We both know you don't know anything about design, and nothing riles my people like someone who doesn't know his hat from a hole in the ground telling them how to do their jobs. We're good at what we do, and we're going to keep on doing it how we've always done it."

If John reacts with little emotional intelligence, he might tend to defend himself and patronize his listener, maybe even use positional authority to win the point. Some examples:

"Your department may be successful, but the process as a whole isn't. I've said this is a priority, so you'd better think about getting involved. Now."

Or:

"You didn't listen to what I said. In fact, you missed my point completely. The whole idea is that we have to shift our focus to a broader view. Just take a look at these figures. . . ."

Or:

"I'm not trying to tell you how to do your job. What I'm trying to tell you is to think beyond your group, for once."

Or, most honestly:

"Now just a minute. I may not know anything about design, but I know when a process doesn't work. And if ever a process doesn't work, it's our supply chain. Last time I looked, Design was a part of that chain, or have you finally seceded and made that little fiefdom you've always wanted?"

These responses would all alienate the head of the Design department, making him determined to stand his ground and negating any possibility of his support. Equally important, they would not convey John's very real desire to have the listener's support—and the support of others who might agree with his point of view. Instead, these responses hide the vulnerability that is the ground for that desire, the place where humans might make connection and move into an authentic dialogue.

How can John realize other options? By first recognizing his emotional reaction, and then moving himself one step away from it, through acknowledgment. As with resistance, openly acknowledging a feeling defuses it and allows us to get to a deeper place, to get the feeling in perspective rather than reacting to it. From there, we can offer the truth, a logical and emotional response that is more complete, more authentic, without giving up any conviction. One way of doing this might be:

"I'm trying not to be defensive here—although I have to admit, not very successfully. I don't want to tell you how to do your job, and at the same time, I want your support and it feels like I'm not getting it. That worries me.

I really believe we want the same thing, to make a major impact on the efficiency of the company, to have that recognized for what it is, and to satisfy customers. Obviously you are good at what you do; that's not at issue here at all. I do think that there's some real value for all of us to at least examine looking at how we work with each other down the line. Can you tell me why you're so strongly against it?"

This alternative continues the dialogue by contributing authenticity, the recognition of the emotional impact of the suggested change, and an assumption of good will. All three are components of being emotionally mature; all three are necessary to continue the engagement and move toward a shared commitment.

Performance Appraisal

Often, the most important communication situation for a leader is the performance appraisal process: letting people honestly and candidly know how they are performing. This is a vital communication skill in major change efforts, as people tend to drag their feet or need reinforcement from the leader to continue the change process.

Not surprisingly, performance measurement is reported as the most onerous communication required of business leaders, particularly during times of rapid change. It is the forced breaking of convention—a time in which we are supposed to tell the truth in order to rate someone's performance and help them improve. But few want to do that. In business, companies struggle with getting appraisals completed on time, and when they do, they struggle with compression at the top of the curve, with far more people being rated "A" or "exceeds requirements" than "D" or "needs substantial improvement." As a result, when a person's performance deteriorates to a level that requires corrective action, or when a reduction in force requires that a company lay off the weakest performers, few leaders and few employees are prepared for the truth. The weaker performers have not been told the truth, so not infrequently, the person fired has been told, in sequence, "good," "good," "good-bye!" This "good," "good" is the equivalent of social promotion in the school system, and like that phenomenon has a detrimental impact on everyone. The person fired has not been given the honest feedback that might have sparked real improvement, the leader has shirked the responsibility to develop the staff, and those remaining feel the person who left was treated unfairly. And they are right. They also might doubt the importance of their own good appraisal and fear that they might be the next to go.

How could an appraisal be conducted using the models we have offered? Listen to this leader introduce the process to one of his direct reports:

> Tom, this appraisal is a ritual that we perform on a regular basis, and sometimes it can be a difficult one. It really helps if we keep the purpose in mind. We're here to make sure that you and I see eye-to-eye on your performance, and to help you to continue to improve and develop so you can grow your career.
>
> I wouldn't be surprised if you were nervous about it. Sometimes being graded doesn't feel so good. Truthfully, in the past, this has not been my favorite activity either, but as soon as I can see it as a chance to help you rather than a chore I have to perform, I feel differently about it. That point of view also helps me see any criticism I might offer as constructive rather than hurtful or personal. It is my intent to be helpful in this process, not just to give my personal opinion of how you've done.
>
> What I thought we could do is to review briefly where we've been, take a look at your plan from last year, our expec-

tations that we set down, then review where we are, how you've performed against the benchmarks, and then spend some time looking to the . . . future—where you want to go. Then at the end, we can make some commitments to one another about what we are going to do for the next period. How does that sound?

Just this lead-in conversation sets up the framework discussion. This leader has established some trust by being clear about purpose, acknowledging some resistance, and relating his own personal motivation. Then he has suggested that the two create a shared context by reviewing the "story" as they have seen it, which will be the main part of the appraisal. He has also suggested a look to the future, and the certainty of making commitments to one another to help bring that future about. If the leader is able to direct the conversation, maintaining his own emotional control, the interview can result in a positive outcome for both.

Mail and E-Mail Reinforcement

In Chapter Ten you read an example of Ross Dove's Chairman's Letter. Ross earned the right to communicate this way by frequently putting himself face to face with the people in the company. That is an important caveat. Mail and e-mail are removed from human contact, and as such they can seem sterile and inflexible. As noted in Chapter One, these modes of communication can breed ambiguity, particularly about the intention of the sender. But if you as leader have established your trustworthiness and competence personally, by deploying yourself generously with those you wish to inspire, these modes can be used effectively to reinforce your message. The better people know you personally, the more likely they will be to fill in whatever they need to make your message effective on both of these levels. To test this theory, imagine an e-mail message from a new HR executive telling you that he wants to discuss your job performance with you, versus the same one from your boss of five years.

One creates anxiety, the other seems much more routine. Spouses who have lived together for thirty years barely have to talk to understand one another. Conversely, lawyers in a courtroom have to cover every detail. One communication requires practically no context, and the other requires very high context; every word must be defined.

Given these considerations, the crafting of e-mail has to be carefully considered if the entire message is to get across. Even leaders who have already earned the trust of their constituents have to include a range of content consistent with their message platform.

Here is one from a Fortune 500 CEO that follows a personal announcement about the need to restructure, a difficult message:

> Today, I'm announcing further steps in the difficult but necessary process of restructuring our company to succeed in this extremely challenging business environment. While I spoke to all of you yesterday about this, I want to reiterate some of what I said.
>
> First, this is necessary because of the changing needs of our clients, and our commitment to continue our heritage of providing the services and products that they find most useful. As the leader in moving the industry in new directions, we simply have to be the most responsive, keeping our clients, our shareholders, and most of all, you, confident of our long-term success.
>
> Obviously this is not easy. Our messages may feel contradictory sometimes. It may appear we are both going forwards and backwards at the same time. In some sense this is true. Even as we charge ahead with new capabilities and offerings that are attracting attention and winning in the marketplace, we also have to go backwards and clean up some of the overcapacity we built in the past for a different era.

This note went on to cover more specifics, but the leader first reiterated what he had said personally, and then once again, acknowledged some obvious resistance: that the messages might seem contradictory, growing in some areas but shrinking in others. Because this leader had addressed the issues personally, he could use e-mail to support his change process. The same rules can be applied to other kinds of indirect communication. Consider carefully what the listeners might not know, or might not remember—including your own motivation—rather than assuming that they know and accept everything.

Follow-up conversation, performance appraisal, and electronic reinforcement are all inevitable in change initiatives. They call for the leader's best: self-awareness, self-control, and empathy. With these three, even the most difficult and complex communication can be productive.

Notes

Chapter One

1. L. Uchitelle, "The Rise of the Losing Class," *New York Times*, section 4 (November 20, 1994): 1.

2. W.V.D. Wishard, "Between Two Ages—Get Used to It," presentation at the Coudert Institute, Palm Beach, Florida, December 1, 2001.

3. M. Wheatley, *Leadership and the New Science* (San Francisco: Berrett-Koehler, 1992), p. 150.

4. M. Parris, "Don't Prompt Me, I'm Speaking," *London Times* (October 6, 1993): 14.

5. E. M. Hallowell, "The Human Moment at Work," *Harvard Business Review* (January-February 1999): 58.

6. C. Handy, *The Age of Unreason* (Boston: Harvard Business School Press, 1990), p. 135.

Chapter Two

1. W. Bennis and others, "Learning Some Basic Truisms About Leadership," in *The New Paradigm in Business*, edited by M. Ray and A. Rinzler (New York: Putnam, 1993), p. 77.

2. W. Bennis, *On Becoming a Leader* (Boston: Addison-Wesley, 1992), p. 122.

3. M. Cuomo, *More Than Words: The Speeches of Mario Cuomo* (New York: St. Martin's Press, 1993), pp. xvi, xviii.

4. J. Hillman and M. Ventura, *We've Had a Hundred Years of Psychotherapy—and the World's Getting Worse* (San Francisco: Harper San Francisco, 1992), p. 53.

5. H. Schultz and D. J. Yang, *Pour Your Heart Into It* (New York: Hyperion, 1997), pp. 3, 4.

Chapter Three

1. D. Walcott, *Collected Poems 1948–1984* (New York: Farrar, Straus and Giroux, 1986), p. 328.

2. M. Cuomo, *More Than Words: The Speeches of Mario Cuomo* (New York: St. Martin's Press, 1993), p. xvii.

3. R. Commanday, "Repin Flawless in Technique," *San Francisco Chronicle* "Datebook" (December 12, 1992): 32.

Chapter Four

1. D. S. Pottruck and T. Pearce, *Clicks and Mortar: Passion Driven Growth in an Internet Driven World* (San Francisco: Jossey-Bass, 2000), pp. 92–93.

2. D. Goleman, *Emotional Intelligence* (New York: Bantam Books, 1995), p. 28.

3. J. Collins, *Good to Great: Why Some Companies Make the Leap . . . and Others Don't* (New York: HarperBusiness, 2001), p. 74.

Chapter Five

1. For more general discussion of brain function as it relates to human connection, see R. K. Cooper and A. Sawaf, *Executive EQ* (New York: Grosset Putnam, 1996), and T. Lewis, F. Amini, and R. Lannon, *A General Theory of Love* (New York: Random House, 2000).

2. Lewis, Amini, and Lannon, *A General Theory of Love*, p. 64.

3. M. J. Wheatley, "Spiritual Leadership," *Executive Excellence* 19, no. 9 (Sept. 2002): 5.

4. D. Goldin, "The Light of a New Age," *Vital Speeches of the Day* 58, no. 24 (1992): 741.

5. T. Wirth, "Global Conditions," National Press Club speech presented in Washington, D.C., July 12, 1994.

6. For a thorough discussion of metaphor as descriptor of business, see G. Morgan, *Images of Organization* (Thousand Oaks, Calif.: Sage, 1997).

7. R. Mahoney, "Politics, Technology, and Economic Growth," *Vital Speeches of the Day* 59, no. 20 (1993): 627.

8. J. Martin and M. E. Power, "Organizational Stories: More Vivid and Persuasive Than Quantitative Data," in *Psychological Foundations of Organizational Behavior*, edited by B. M. Staw (Glenview, Ill.: Scott, Foresman, 1982), 161–168; also see J. M. Kouzes and B. P. Posner, *Credibility: How Leaders Gain and Lose It, Why People Demand It* (San Francisco: Jossey-Bass, 1993).

Chapter Six

1. F. D. Raines, "Racial Inequality in America," *Vital Speeches of the Day* 68, no. 13 (2002): 400.

2. R. S. Butler, "Planning for Death in a Century of Cure," speech presented at the Haas School of Business, Berkeley, California, March 22, 2002.

3. E. Kennedy, "Eliminating the Threat: The Right Course of Action for Disarming Iraq, Combating Terrorism, Protecting the Homeland, and Stabilizing the Middle East," Sept. 27, 2002; from http:// Kennedy.senate.gov/kennedy/statements/02/09/2002927718.html.

4. R. K. Cooper and A. Sawaf, *Executive EQ* (New York: Grosset Putnam, 1996), p. 100.

5. B. Jordan, videotaped speech (New York: National Broadcasting Company, 1997).

6. M. Cuomo, *More Than Words: The Speeches of Mario Cuomo* (New York: St. Martin's Press, 1993), p. 35.

Chapter Seven

1. H. Nouwen, *The Genesee Diary* (New York: Image Books, 1976), p. 113.

2. S. J. Gould, "The Strike That Was High and Outside," *New York Times*, section 1 (November 19, 1984): 23.

3. P. Senge, *The Fifth Discipline: The Art and Practice of the Learning Organization* (New York: Doubleday, 1990), p. 354.

4. J. Adams, "Juggling Job and Family," *Vital Speeches of the Day* 60, no. 4 (1994): 125.

5. A. Roddick, "Corporate Responsibility," *Vital Speeches of the Day* 60, no. 7 (1994): 197.

6. B. Moyers, *Healing and the Mind* (audiocassette) (Bantam Books Audio, February 1993).

7. R. S. Butler, "Planning for Death in a Century of Cure," speech presented at the Haas School of Business, Berkeley, California, March 22, 2002.

Chapter Eight

1. B. Gwertzman, "The Official View on Iceland Is Still Chilly, but Thawing," *New York Times*, section 4 (October 19, 1986): 1.

2. O. Wilde, *The Wit and Wisdom of Oscar Wilde* (New York: Dover, 1959).

3. A. de Saint-Exupéry, *The Wisdom of the Sands* (French title *Citadelle*), translated by S. Gilbert (Orlando, Fla.: Harcourt Brace, 1950), section 89.

4. Quoted in J. C. Collins and J. I. Porras, *Built to Last* (New York: HarperBusiness, 1994), p. 231.

5. Text of speech available online at http://www.whitehouse.gov/news/releases/2002/09/20020912-1.html; access date: December 2002.

Chapter Nine

1. R. W. Terry, *Authentic Leadership: Courage in Action* (San Francisco: Jossey-Bass, 1993), p. 13.

2. G. W. Bush, *Vital Speeches of the Day* 67, no. 24 (2001): 763.

3. M. Avallone, *A Woman Called Golda* (New York: Leisure Books, 1982), pp. 164–165.

Appendix A

1. A. Clausi, "U.S. Food System Needs for the Twenty-First Century," *Vital Speeches of the Day* 60, no. 17 (1994): 542.

Recommended Reading

Those interested in the subjects discussed in the book can find further value in the following readings. This list is by no means complete, but is representative of publications that I have found most helpful in my own work.

Leadership and Leadership Communication

Cooper, R. and Sawaf, A. *Executive EQ*. New York: Grosset-Putnam, 1997.

Goleman, D., Boyatzis, R., and McKee, A. *Primal Leadership: Realizing the Power of Emotional Intelligence*. Boston: Harvard Business School Press, 2002.

Heifitz, R. *Leadership Without Easy Answers*. Cambridge, Mass.: Belknap Press of Harvard University Press, 1994.

Kouzes, J., and Posner, B. *The Leadership Challenge*. (3rd ed.) San Francisco: Jossey-Bass, 2002.

Lewis, T., Amini, F., and Lannon, R. *A General Theory of Love*. New York: Random House, 2000.

Pottruck, D. and Pearce, T. *Clicks and Mortar: Passion-Driven Growth in an Internet-Driven World*. San Francisco: Jossey-Bass, 2000.

Terry, R. W. *Authentic Leadership: Courage in Action*. San Francisco: Jossey-Bass, 1993.

Organizational Effectiveness

Morgan, G. *Images of Organizations*. Thousand Oaks, Calif.: Sage, 1997.

Neuhauser, P. *Tribal Warfare in Organizations*. New York: HarperBusiness, 1988.

Senge, P. *The Fifth Discipline: The Art and Practice of the Learning Organization*. New York: Doubleday, 1990.

Personal Development and Change

Frankl, V. E. *Man's Search for Meaning*. New York: Pocket Books, 1963.

Gardner, J. W. *Self-Renewal: The Individual and Innovative Society*. (Reissued ed.) New York: Norton, 1995. (Originally published 1963.)

Goleman, D. *Emotional Intelligence*. New York: Bantam Books, 1995.

Leonard, G. *Mastery: The Keys to Long-Term Success and Fulfillment*. New York: Dutton, 1991.

Miller, W. C. *Flash of Brilliance*. New York: Perseus Books, 1999.

Osborn, D. (ed.) *Reflections on the Art of Living: A Joseph Campbell Companion*. New York: HarperCollins, 1991.

Quinn, R. *Deep Change: Discovering the Leader Within*. San Francisco: Jossey-Bass, 1996.

Steindl-Rast, D. *Gratefulness, the Heart of Prayer*. Mahwah, N.J.: Paulist Press, 1984.

Whyte, D. *The Heart Aroused: Poetry and Preservation of the Soul in Corporate America*. New York: Currency/Doubleday, 1994.

Context, Personal and Social

Campbell, J. *The Hero with a Thousand Faces*. (2nd ed.) Princeton N.J.: Princeton University Press, 1973.

Collins, B. (Poet Laureate, 2002). *Sailing Alone Around the Room*. New York: Random House, 2001.

Friedman, T. *The Lexus and the Olive Tree*. New York: Farrar, Straus & Giroux, 1999.

Gergen, K. *The Saturated Self: Dilemmas of Identity in Contemporary Life*. New York: Basic Books, 1991.

Handy, C. *The Age of Unreason*. Boston: Harvard Business School Press, 1990.

Handy, C. *The Hungry Spirit*. New York: Broadway Books, 1998.

Shenk, D. *Data Smog: Surviving the Information Glut*. San Francisco, Harper Edge, 1997.

Tarnas, R. *The Passion of the Western Mind: Understanding the Ideas That Have Shaped Our World View*. New York: Harmony Books: 1991.

Taylor, J., and Wacker, W. *The 500-Year Delta*. New York: HarperBusiness, 1997.

Wishard, W.V.D. *Between Two Ages: The Twenty-First Century and the Crisis of Meaning*. Reston, Va.: WorldTrends Research, 2000.

Finally, for anyone interested in the philosophical foundations, I recommend the following. They are all contemporary, and could supplement any of the more classic philosophical and spiritual texts. Again, the list is not meant to be complete, but representative.

Keen, S. *The Passionate Life: Stages of Loving*. San Francisco: Harper San Francisco, 1983.

Milosz, C. (ed.). *A Book of Luminous Things*. Orlando, Fla.: Harcourt Brace & Company, 1996.

Mitchell, S. (ed.). *The Enlightened Heart*. New York: HarperCollins, 1989.

Mitchell, S. (ed.). *The Enlightened Mind*. New York: HarperCollins, 1991.

Needleman, J. *Money and the Meaning of Life*. New York: Doubleday, 1991.

Needleman, J. *A Little Book on Love*. New York: Doubleday/Currency, 1996.

Needleman, J. *Time and the Soul*. New York: Doubleday/Currency, 1996.

Rilke, R. M. *Letters to a Young Poet*. (S. Mitchell, trans.) New York. Vintage Books, 1986.

Wilber, K. *Up from Eden*. Boston: Shambhala, 1983.

Wilber, K. *A Brief History of Everything*. Boston: Shambhala, 1996.

Acknowledgments

Soon after the original version of this title was published, Christy Tonge expanded the ideas and reshaped *Leading Out Loud* from its book-type cocoon into a butterfly. She transformed the mere text to a program for executives and managers that has made a difference in the way thousands communicate. Other friends at BlessingWhite have continued that transformation process to this day, and all their work is represented in this new edition. Kim Soskin, in particular, was critical to the development of the course as well as to the writing of this new edition. She cajoled, edited, and actually wrote portions of the last chapter on day-to-day application of the principles. She is also a great friend and simply the best communications coach that I know.

Peter Alduino, Sharon Landes, Jeff Rosenthal, and the students at the University of California Haas School of Business and the London Business School have contributed immensely to the expansion and intellectual integrity of the work, as have the many executives who have attended courses in the concepts at these institutions and elsewhere. Thanks particularly to Costas Markidos of the London Business School for sponsorship and friendship.

Those who shared their stories brought the ideas to life. Thanks to John Ure, Tom Murphy, Ed Jensen, Karen Chang, Josie Gaillard, Rebekah Saul Butler, and Gary Fiedel.

To my best friend and partner, Dave Pottruck, and his wife, Emily Scott-Pottruck, I offer my intense gratitude, my greatest thanks. Dave's personal use and sponsorship of the principles of *Leading Out Loud* has amplified their value. It has taken personal courage for him to do that, and I appreciate it.

Jan Hunter is no ordinary developmental editor; rather she is a contributor, substantively and spiritually, to everyone on the project, everything that is written. Her character and her incredible talent are hard to overstate, and I am lucky to count her as counselor. Hilary Powers added her magic at the end with precision copyedits and suggestions that vastly improved the flow of ideas. And the folks at Jossey-Bass just make it easy. My thanks go particularly to Rob Brandt, Byron Schneider, Susan Williams, and Jeff Wyneken.

Sue Porter ran our company, contributed to the content, inspired my own writing, and put up with bad temper during the process. To her, a great Huzzah! Lisa Kemp researched, tracked down citations, and contributed her substantial energy to all of us, while Mehrnaz Hosseini gave us a great lift in the final days of preparation. Thank you.

This new edition was actually more difficult to write than the original. It required a particularly difficult discipline to see and to distinguish what is new from what was a restatement. It takes special people to put up with and contribute to the kind of craziness it requires to see this process through, and I am blessed with many such patient people in my life. To associates and friends—Linda Stoick, Mark Thompson, Paul Burns, Leni Miller, Darlene Anaman-Perry, James Murrow, Isa Foulk, Katherine Zsolt, Gene Stone, Ralph Tolson, and Jim McNeil—thanks for not leaving.

To Karen Anderson DiFrancesca—for love and support despite the stress, for late-night dinners, long phone calls, and laserlike edits—many hugs of gratitude.

And finally to my family . . . Jeff and Alissa, Joel and Jen, Jodi and Jason, and to all of their kiddles, my deepest love.

T.P.

About the Author

Terry Pearce is founder and president of Leadership Communication, a company that coaches high-profile corporate, political, and social leaders. The content and method of his coaching are radical departures from conventional wisdom, and are designed to move people to commitment rather than mere compliance, inspiring new levels of contribution and innovation. His clients include top executives and executive teams of Fortune 500 companies. Terry is also a lecturer at the Haas Business School at the University of California, Berkeley, where his courses receive the highest ratings from graduate students for providing useful, effective, and relevant tools for their futures as leaders in the business community. He is a visiting lecturer at the London School of Business, a contributor to the Executive Briefing Video Series at Stanford University, and a project consultant and interviewer for the CD series, "Leaders of the New Century." Terry is a frequent keynote speaker in the United States and abroad.

His avid interest and commitment to the relationship between leadership and communication began as a student leader at Linfield College in Oregon where he earned a B.S. degree in business with an emphasis in religious philosophy. For the first seventeen years of his career, Terry was a manager and executive at IBM. During the 1980s he pioneered U.S. business activities in the Soviet Union as co-founder of Partners, which continues to market consumer products and facilitate joint industrial projects in Russia. From 1994 until 2002, he also served as a fellow and a senior vice president of executive communication for Charles Schwab & Co., Inc.

Terry's other writings include the business best-seller *Clicks and Mortar: Passion-Driven Growth in an Internet-Driven World* (co-authored with David Pottruck) and *Leading Out Loud: The Authentic Speaker, the Credible Leader,* hailed by "Executive Summaries" as one of the thirty best business books of 1995, and as "one of the best books on speaking ever written."

Active in the community, Terry was the founding director of the Partnership for a Drug-Free California, and in 1989 ran across the United States as a member of "Transcon 89" to promote this cause. He currently serves on the boards of the Pottruck Family Foundation and the National Endowment for Financial Education.

He has three grown children and lives in Northern California.

Index

Terry Pearce
Leadership Communication™

Leading Out Loud is the basis for Terry Pearce's graduate courses at the University of California Haas School of Business and the London Business School, and is taught by others at several universities around the world. Terry also teaches the principles of *Leading Out Loud* in a number of different formats, including one-on-one leadership coaching and intensive workshops through his company, Leadership Communication, and in partnership with BlessingWhite.

If you are interested in more information about leadership coaching, about using this book as the basis for a university course, or if you have stories of inspirational communication you would like to share, please call us at 800-658-4453 or visit our virtual home at http://www. terrypearce.com.

 Terry Pearce
Leadership Communication™

You've Read the Book, What's Next?

For thirty years, BlessingWhite has helped organizations reinvent leadership and the meaning of work. Through our partnership with Terry Pearce, we are privileged to offer a workshop designed to help organizations

- Create authentic leaders who inspire committed action.
- Raise the standard for the candid, constructive conversations that spur innovation throughout organizations.

To learn more about the Leading Out Loud™ workshop, call us at 1-800-222-1349 or visit us at http://www.blessingwhite.com.

BlessingWhite

Reinventing Leadership and the Meaning of Work™